Elements of
Language

Chapter Tests

- Reading
- Writing
- Sentences and Paragraphs
- Grammar, Usage, Mechanics

HOLT, RINEHART AND WINSTON

A Harcourt Education Company

Orlando • **Austin** • New York • San Diego • London

Table of Contents

About These Tests v
Symbols for Revising and Proofreading vi

Grammar, Usage, and Mechanics

for PART 1

(Student Edition pp. 46–507)

Chapter 1: Parts of Speech Overview 1
Chapter 2: The Parts of a Sentence 4
Chapter 3: The Phrase 7
Chapter 4: The Clause 10
Chapter 5: Agreement 13
Chapter 6: Using Pronouns Correctly 16
Chapter 7: Clear Reference 19
Chapter 8: Using Verbs Correctly 22
Chapter 9: Using Modifiers Correctly 25
Chapter 10: Placement of Modifiers 28
Chapter 11: A Glossary of Usage 31
Chapter 12: Capitalization 34
Chapter 13: Punctuation
End Marks and Commas 37
Chapter 14: Punctuation
Other Marks of Punctuation 40
Chapter 15: Spelling 43
Chapter 16: Correcting Common Errors 46

Sentences and Paragraphs

for PART 2

(Student Edition pp. 508–585)

Chapter 17: Writing Clear Sentences 49
Chapter 18: Combining Sentences 52
Chapter 19: Improving Sentence Style 55
Chapter 20: Understanding Paragraphs and Compositions 58

Table of Contents

Communications

for PART 3

(Student Edition pp. 587–989)

Chapter 21: Narration/Description
Remembering People
Reading Workshop **61**
Writing Workshop **64**

Chapter 22: Narration/Description
Harnessing Your Imagination
Reading Workshop **67**
Writing Workshop **72**

Chapter 23: Exposition
Comparing and Contrasting Media
Reading Workshop **75**
Writing Workshop **76**

Chapter 24: Exposition
Analyzing Causal Relationships
Reading Workshop **81**
Writing Workshop **84**

Chapter 25: Exposition
Analyzing Drama
Reading Workshop **87**
Writing Workshop **90**

Chapter 26: Exposition
Researching Literary Subjects
Reading Workshop **93**
Writing Workshop **96**

Chapter 27: Persuasion
Defending a Position
Reading Workshop **99**
Writing Workshop **102**

Chapter 28: Persuasion
Reviewing a Documentary
Reading Workshop **105**
Writing Workshop **108**

Chapter 29: Persuasion
Recommending Solutions
Reading Workshop **111**
Writing Workshop **114**

About These Tests

Every chapter in your *Elements of Language* Student Edition has an accompanying Chapter Test in traditional format. The Answer Keys for these tests are located on the *Teacher One Stop*.

Part 1 **Grammar, Usage, and Mechanics**

The Part 1 tests provide assessment for the rules and key concepts taught in the grammar, usage, and mechanics chapters in the Student Edition. Students demonstrate their mastery of the instruction by completing a variety of tests that are similar to the exercises in the Student Edition.

Part 2 **Sentences and Paragraphs**

The Part 2 tests provide assessment for each major section within the Sentences and Paragraphs chapters. Students complete exercises similar to those in the Student Edition. These exercises test students' mastery of the key concepts taught in the chapters.

Part 3 **Communications**

The Part 3 tests include assessment for both the Reading and the Writing Workshops. You may choose to administer the Reading and Writing Workshop tests separately or as one test after students have completed the chapter.

In the **Reading Workshop** test, students read a passage, respond to short-answer questions, and complete a graphic organizer. The passage is in the mode that students have just studied, and the questions and the graphic organizer assess students' proficiency in the chapter's Reading Skill and Reading Focus.

The **Writing Workshop** test provides a passage containing problems or errors in several or all of the following areas: content, organization, style, grammar and usage, and mechanics. Students demonstrate their understanding of the mode of writing and their revising and proofreading skills by revising the essay and correcting the errors. A Revising Guidelines page reminds students of the chapter skills and the basic requirements of the chapter writing mode.

To help students complete the Writing Workshop tests, you may want to give them photocopies of the following page, which lists symbols for revising and proofreading.

Symbols for Revising and Proofreading

The following symbols will help you revise and correct the passages in the
Writing Workshop tests.

▶ SYMBOL	▶ DEFINITION	▶ EXAMPLE
___ ℛ	Delete word.	The girl smiled ~~at me.~~
∧	Insert.	The girl smiled. *at me*
∧___	Replace a word.	I found the ~~book.~~ *record*
≡	Set in capital letters.	Does karen like fish?
/	Set in lowercase.	Does Karen Like Fish?
ˇ	Insert apostrophe.	Its his dog.
ˇˇ	Insert quotation marks.	It's his dog, he said.
⊙	Insert period.	If she goes, I go
˄	Insert comma.	If she goes I go.
⊙	Insert colon.	Pick a color ed, blue, or green.
˄	Insert semicolon.	We went she stayed.

   ELEMENTS OF LANGUAGE | Sixth Course

Parts of Speech Overview: Identification and Function

A. IDENTIFYING TYPES OF NOUNS AND PRONOUNS   Each of the following sentences is followed by the names of one kind of noun and one kind of pronoun in parentheses. In the sentence, underline each example of that kind of noun once and each example of that kind of pronoun twice.

Example 1. The people who favored Puritanism wanted worship services that were simpler and more morally strict. (*abstract noun, relative pronoun*)

1. With extra money from odd jobs, Kevin treated himself to a trip to Minnesota to see his new nephew. (*proper noun, reflexive pronoun*)

2. If anyone wants to feed the manatees, he or she may throw some lettuce into the water for them. (*concrete noun, indefinite pronoun*)

3. Is this the toolbox that you want to buy for Aunt Sarah, or is that the one? (*compound noun, demonstrative pronoun*)

4. Frankly, I was surprised when Yvette told me that she was to have the honor of representing the school for all of us. (*abstract noun, personal pronoun*)

5. The chairperson on the environmental impact committee herself wrote to the attorney general to ask him to work for more antipollution laws. (*compound noun, intensive pronoun*)

6. The jury, which consisted of six women and six men, deliberated for only an hour before reaching its verdict. (*collective noun, relative pronoun*)

7. Who is the man who sells vegetables almost every day near Union Station? (*common noun, interrogative pronoun*)

8. Many in the group talked a lot about integrity, but I think that at least some, maybe even most, of them do not really understand the word. (*abstract noun, indefinite pronoun*)

9. The train rumbled through the village at 3 P.M., but that was not the reason they looked outside then. (*common noun, demonstrative pronoun*)

10. Although Mrs. Baker taught herself Spanish, she has decided to find an instructor who can teach her Russian. (*proper noun, relative pronoun*)

B. IDENTIFYING MAIN VERBS AND VERB PHRASES   Underline the main verb or verb phrase in each of the following sentences. For each verb phrase, circle all helping verbs.

Example 1. You must know about Cozumel, an island off Mexico's Yucatán Peninsula.

11. The island was sacred to the Maya as the home of their mother goddess Ixchel.

12. Interested in Mayan history and culture, a group from the university will be traveling there this spring.

13. The Mayas worshiped at temples and shrines on Cozumel from A.D. 600 to 1500.

14. Visitors can see remains of a few of these ancient structures.

15. The Mexican government has partly restored the temple of San Gervasio.

16. At one time, Cozumel was used by Jean Lafitte and other pirates as a hide-out.

17. Musicians were playing the marimba on the plaza in the town of San Miguel last summer.

18. Do visitors still ride scooters to tour the island?

19. You could read more about the island in guidebooks or magazines.

20. People clearly enjoy the island for many reasons, including exploring, swimming, and snorkeling.

C. IDENTIFYING TYPES OF VERBS Each of the following sentences is followed by the names of two kinds of verbs in parentheses. Circle the name of the kind of verb or verb phrase that is italicized in the sentence.

Example 1. The chamber orchestra's performance of the Mozart sonata *sounded* beautiful. (*action verb* or *linking verb*)

21. The truck *slid* off the road during last night's snowstorm. (*transitive verb* or *intransitive verb*)

22. Michael *rocketed* the ball over the net right past his opponent. (*transitive verb* or *intransitive verb*)

23. The curiosity of the playful cat about the jangling bell eventually *became* greater and greater. (*action verb* or *linking verb*)

24. Mom *rushed* out the back door and into the garden. (*transitive verb* or *intransitive verb*)

25. At the end of the tournament, the winning team *received* a large trophy. (*action verb* or *linking verb*)

26. *Did* Meredith *record* her new song about the nature preserve? (*transitive verb* or *intransitive verb*)

27. That last slice of pizza *should have been* yours. (*action verb* or *linking verb*)

28. Three times during the last month I *have dreamed* about the characters in that movie. (*action verb* or *linking verb*)

29. Ashley *yelled* to her brother, who was watching the parade approaching them. (*transitive verb* or *intransitive verb*)

30. Without any good clues, the trio *could* only *speculate* about the meaning of the riddle. (*action verb* or *linking verb*)

D. **IDENTIFYING PARTS OF SPEECH** The following sentences contain italicized words and word groups. Above each italicized word or word group, identify its part of speech. Use the following abbreviations: *ADJ* for *adjective*, *ADV* for *adverb*, *PREP* for *preposition*, *CONJ* for *conjunction*, *INT* for *interjection*, *N* for *noun*, *PN* for *pronoun*, *V* for *verb*.

Example 1. Dorothy stayed *home* tonight *so that* she could finish writing her *essay*.
                     ADV   CONJ   N

31. Ms. Lee's new job is *quite* lucrative, *and* it's also most *enjoyable*, she says.

32. *Although* we've seen *It's a Wonderful Life* several times *before*, we *want* to see it again.

33. *Oh*, the *questions* went on far *too* long, and our team didn't know *many* answers.

34. *Many* of the games have been rescheduled *according to* the radio *announcer*.

35. After the workers *cemented* the blocks in place, they *took* an *afternoon* break.

36. *Since* Joan couldn't tell *which* coat was mine, she brought *both* of them to me.

37. Perhaps *each* boy will want his own canoe, but that may *not* be *possible*.

38. The bear left *its* den and *lazily* headed for *the* pond.

39. *Wow*, did you see that the museum paid *millions* of dollars for *those* fake watercolors?

40. The chipmunks took the *piece* of bread and ran *away*, and we haven't seen them *since*.

41. The confused children *asked* the *salesclerk* at the register *next to* the entrance for directions to the game room.

42. "*This* is an interesting book *that* Amelia gave me; it's a novel set in the *Middle Ages*."

43. A *cheerful* outlook *can* help to make difficult *situations* bearable.

44. *Which* of the trees *bears* the *most* fruit?

45. "*Something* is supposed to happen *during* class today, but I can't remember *what* it is," Cole said.

46. *If* I order a *bean* burrito, will I have *enough* time to eat it?

47. The soloist played extremely *well* in the recital, *yet* she said later that *she* had been scared.

48. *Two* horses galloped *past* the fence *as if* they owned the arena.

49. *Yes*, it's certain that *either* Lucien *or* Timothy will be chosen for the *part*.

50. Could you really *part* with *your* collection of *baseball* cards?

The Parts of a Sentence: Subject, Predicate, Complement

A. IDENTIFYING SENTENCES   Identify each of the following groups of words as a sentence or a sentence fragment. On the line provided, write *S* for *sentence* or *F* for *fragment.*

Example __*F*__ **1.** The Tallgrass Prairie Preserve located in Oklahoma.

_______ **1.** Consisting of thirty-five thousand acres of tallgrass prairie land north of Tulsa.

_______ **2.** In fact, it is the largest tallgrass prairie.

_______ **3.** When three hundred bison were released there in 1993.

_______ **4.** Before Europeans settled the area, bison and thousands of other species lived on

the prairie.

_______ **5.** A kind of grass called big bluestem, which can grow as high as ten feet.

_______ **6.** Wasn't plowed up like many prairies because ranchers, not farmers, settled there.

_______ **7.** The Nature Conservancy now operates the preserve.

_______ **8.** With support from Osage Indians, ranchers, and oil producers in the area.

_______ **9.** Mineral rights to the land give the Osage added income.

_______ **10.** Scientific study of the evolution of the land and the future of the prairie.

B. IDENTIFYING SUBJECTS AND PREDICATES   In each of the following sentences, underline the complete subject once and the complete predicate twice. Then, circle the simple subject and the simple predicate. A simple subject or a simple predicate may be compound. If a sentence has an understood subject, write it above the first word in the sentence.

Example 1. There may be two regular evening performances and a benefit matinee of the new

opera based on the novel *Little Women.*

11. Will you please answer the next question?

12. T. J. and Miranda probably will try the new restaurant before deciding whether to have their

party there.

13. Up in the attic were stored many boxes of my parents' keepsakes.

14. The Orinoco is a river in Venezuela, flowing from the border of Brazil into the Atlantic.

15. Outside the front entrance to the cathedral, Spencer and Melinda waited for their friends.

16. The crocodiles slithered across the marsh and slipped into the open water.

17. No one recalls hearing the announcement the first time.

18. Tomas had read a few novels by African writers but had never heard of Chinua Achebe.

19. The boys on the team jogged to the mall and then ran back.

20. In Buddhism, one title of respect and reverence is *mahatma*.

21. The bus filled with band members arrived at the stadium an hour before the game.

22. The window trim, all of the doors, and even the mailbox are painted blue.

23. The smell of the freshly baked biscuits delighted the early risers on the campout.

24. Both languages, Japanese and Chinese, interest me and are offered at the university.

25. Please watch the toaster.

26. The intercultural committee met yesterday and voted to begin a promotional media campaign.

27. There seekers may discover the missing jewels.

28. In what state did the Dred Scott trial begin?

29. The old iron bars and the metal railings were thrown into the scrapheap.

30. Have Miss Simmons and her fiancé already reserved the mansion and hired caterers for their

wedding reception?

C. IDENTIFYING KINDS OF COMPLEMENTS　Identify which kind of complement is italicized in each of the
following sentences. Above each italicized word or word group, write *DO* for *direct object*, *IO* for *indirect
object*, *PN* for *predicate nominative*, *PA* for *predicate adjective*, or *OC* for *objective complement*.

　　　　　　　　　　　　　　　　　　　　　　　　　　　　　OC
Example 1. At least three newspapers have called the song *brilliant*.

31. With patience and compassion, Philip calmed the frightened *burros* during the storm.

32. The states in which I've lived are *Texas, Arkansas,* and *Missouri*.

33. Let's buy *Ernesto* some macadamia nuts from Hawaii.

34. People often find telemarketing calls *annoying* and *bothersome*.

35. My parents have decided *to give away anything they haven't used within the last five years.*

36. The owner of the bookstore handed *Dora* and *Gretchen* each a copy of the Dalai Lama's

new book.

37. The pumpkin pie tastes *spicy* and *delicious*.

38. "We need *you* in Washington!" shouted the candidate's enthusiastic supporters.

39. One of the most glorious feelings I've enjoyed all my life has been *to swing back and forth*

at the playground on a sunny spring afternoon.

40. Unfortunately, the twins consider the toys *theirs*.

41. Marianne's brother spends some *time* at the gym several days a week.

42. The church's rose window looks truly *beautiful*.

43. "I will discard *what I've written* and start over," Cynthia said.

44. Count Basie is his favorite jazz *performer*.

45. Ray's diligent work garnered *him* special recognition at the Student Achievements Banquet.

46. The principal, who enjoys rewarding good students, named Mack *"Principal for a Day."*

47. She should give *whoever most appreciates them* her prized plants.

48. *Who* are the new residents of apartment 318?

49. Do the dogs like their new *house, lawn,* and shade *trees*?

50. The tense relations slowly turned more *amicable* and *pleasant*.

for **CHAPTER 3** `page 104`   **CHAPTER TEST**

The Phrase: Kinds of Phrases and Their Functions

A. IDENTIFYING AND CLASSIFYING PREPOSITIONAL PHRASES In each of the following sentences, underline each prepositional phrase, and draw an arrow to the word it modifies. Then, classify each prepositional phrase by writing *ADJ* for *adjective phrase* or *ADV* for *adverb phrase* on the line provided.

Example *ADV, ADJ, ADV* **1.** In the East African country of Uganda is a unique forest that is popular with gorilla watchers.

1. Part of the forest extends into the Bwindi Impenetrable National Park.

2. The park, established in 1991, lies near the border between Uganda and the Democratic Republic of the Congo.

3. The park teems with vegetation that grows lavishly across its hills and valleys.

4. In addition to its vegetation, the park provides safe haven for a stunning variety of animals.

5. Within the park and along its perimeter lives a large percentage of the world's mountain-gorilla population.

6. People come from all over the world to see gorillas.

7. Uganda's financial situation, at one time diminished after political unrest, improved because of the park tourism.

8. Gorilla enthusiasts, led by guides, gather in the park each morning to walk the trails.

9. A magazine article about Bwindi states that chimpanzees also live there along with the gorillas.

10. The largest town near Bwindi is Kabale, which is a three-hour trip away over dirt roads.

B. IDENTIFYING VERBAL PHRASES Identify the kind of verbal phrase that is italicized in each of the following sentences. On the line provided, write *PART* for *participial phrase*, *GER* for *gerund phrase*, or *INF* for *infinitive phrase*.

Example *PART* **1.** With its mane and tail *flying in the wind*, the horse raced across the pasture.

11. *Built out of pink granite*, the museum's walls are not only sturdy but also showy.

12. *To have lived during the Renaissance* would have thrilled Robin.

______ **13.** Sherry realized that yesterday, *being so sunny and dry*, would be a perfect day to mow the lawn.

______ **14.** The senator's main interest has always been *helping people help themselves*.

______ **15.** *Amazed by the actor's versatility*, the audience began applauding after watching only a few minutes of the skit.

______ **16.** My parents planned *to leave the car at the airport*.

______ **17.** Cousin Kelly earns a surprising amount of money from her part-time job, which is *teaching people how to navigate the Web*.

______ **18.** Uncle George was delighted *to have been invited*.

______ **19.** *Having read the newspaper thoroughly*, Jonas put it in the recycling box.

______ **20.** In his spare time, my science teacher enjoys *photographing wildlife*.

______ **21.** Do you have enough flour *to make the scones*?

______ **22.** In *responding to your supervisor*, be as polite as you can be.

______ **23.** *Spinning out of control*, the bobsled repeatedly slammed into the wall.

______ **24.** The hungry cyclists made *finding something to eat* their top priority.

______ **25.** *To gain free admission to the park*, we used a coupon we had gotten in the mail.

______ **26.** My young brother, *once stung by a bee*, now refuses to eat honey.

______ **27.** Grace will attend the workshop *to learn better communication skills*.

______ **28.** *Having just gotten her coat back from the dry cleaner*, Elena didn't want to wear it out in the snow.

______ **29.** Anyone *wanting extra credit in the course* should read the book and write a report.

______ **30.** After a busy week, Fran looks forward to *resting on the weekend*.

C. IDENTIFYING APPOSITIVES AND APPOSITIVE PHRASES   Underline the appositive or appositive phrase in each of the following sentences.

Example 1. An inventive and clever boy, Jack wants to be an engineer.

31. Our friend Richard works nights at the city water department.

32. Hector wants to be like his uncle, someone who has traveled all over the world.

33. An alert, small hound, the beagle can be traced as a breed back to ancient Rome.

34. Her business, insurance, is constantly changing, but she finds it stimulating.

35. The lead actress in that new television series is my aunt Laura.

36. Dawn, one of the newborn twins, has red hair like her mother's.

37. My new alarm clock, a gift from my grandparents, is on the bedside table.

38. My ancestors came from Great Grimsby, a seaport in northeast England.

39. Have you met Margaret Martinez, the new recreation-center director?

40. A surprise, the snowstorm slowed rush-hour traffic.

D. IDENTIFYING PHRASES　Identify the kind of phrase that is italicized in each of the following sentences. Write *PREP* for *prepositional phrase*, *PART* for *participial phrase*, *GER* for *gerund phrase*, *INF* for *infinitive phrase*, *ABS* for *absolute phrase*, or *APP* for *appositive phrase* on the line provided.

Example *PART* **1.** Do you see anyone *waving at us from the window?*

_______ **41.** The carpenter looked pleased *to have finished the cabinets so soon.*

_______ **42.** The clocks *throughout the entire school* are set incorrectly, I've noticed.

_______ **43.** Tanya said that, *all things being equal,* she would skip the ceremony.

_______ **44.** Our computer, *a new model,* was actually less expensive than our older one.

_______ **45.** *Practicing their ballroom dance steps,* the beginning students appeared to be having fun.

_______ **46.** When Dad walked in, of course, my brother stopped *teasing me.*

_______ **47.** The school board voted *to repair the parking lot* and now needs to get bids on the cost.

_______ **48.** Their closets are filled with clothes *bought at various sales around town.*

_______ **49.** *Publishing a weekly neighborhood newspaper* is his dream.

_______ **50.** I have homework in Spanish III and history tonight *in addition to my weekly writing assignment* in English.

The Clause: Independent and Subordinate Clauses, Sentence Structure

A. IDENTIFYING INDEPENDENT AND SUBORDINATE CLAUSES For each of the following sentences, identify the italicized clause as independent or subordinate. On the line provided, write *IND* for *independent* or *SUB* for *subordinate*.

Example _SUB_ **1.** That artist gives everyone *who comes to his show* a hand-painted bookmark.

_______ **1.** *When the music stopped*, the children at the birthday party scrambled to the chairs.

_______ **2.** *Marta agreed to go on a date with Chuck* because he has a good sense of humor.

_______ **3.** "Here are the pictures *I've been looking for!*" exclaimed Ansel.

_______ **4.** The statue was moved from in front of the chair *so that no one would trip over it again*.

_______ **5.** I don't know where the train station is, but *I'll find it*.

_______ **6.** There's still time to go to the library, *which is open late on Monday night*.

_______ **7.** *We wonder* whether the basketball game will be telecast locally.

_______ **8.** "*Unless the dishes start washing themselves*, I'd better get busy," Brett joked.

_______ **9.** My English literature book is thicker *than any of my other books*.

_______ **10.** *Li Sue is the one* whose math scores were highest.

B. CLASSIFYING SUBORDINATE CLAUSES On the line provided, classify the kind of subordinate clause that is italicized in the sentence. Write *ADJ* for *adjective clause*, *ADV* for *adverb clause*, or *N* for *noun clause*. For each adjective or adverb clause, circle the word or words that the clause modifies. For each noun clause, identify how it is used in the sentence. Above the noun clause, write *S* for *subject*, *PN* for *predicate nominative*, *DO* for *direct object*, *IO* for *indirect object*, or *OP* for *object of the preposition*.

Example _ADJ_ **1.** There will come a ⟨time⟩, I believe, *when people will understand the futility of conflict*.

_______ **11.** *How music recordings are made* was demonstrated Saturday at the studio.

_______ **12.** The new rug is wider *than our other one*.

_______ **13.** The speech *that Ben gave about his many summer jobs* was better than any other one he has presented.

_______ **14.** *Because you are very conscientious*, you have a better chance at succeeding at whatever you do.

_______ **15.** Her mother used to give *whoever visited her* a small jar of her homemade marmalade.

_______ **16.** Bill's instructor wanted *him to finish the exercises in the electronics manual*.

_______ **17.** Mrs. Alward is the only attorney I know *who has never lost a case*.

_______ **18.** "You can borrow my pens *as long as you return them*," Rick said.

_______ **19.** We asked Mr. Quinn *if we could watch the whole series about the solar system*.

_______ **20.** These seats cost more *than the ones directly behind them do*.

_______ **21.** The preschoolers thought that the story was much funnier *when a hand puppet was used in the telling*.

_______ **22.** The welding class *in which I'm enrolled* has only two more openings.

_______ **23.** Luanna usually works several days a week at the humane society *after school has ended*.

_______ **24.** The money collected will be used for *whatever worthy cause the group selects*.

_______ **25.** "My parents are the ones *whom I most admire*," Sasha said, "and I know I'm fortunate to be able to say that."

_______ **26.** *When driving any vehicle*, focus on what you're doing.

_______ **27.** Her friendly nature is *why Shannon is popular*.

_______ **28.** The Perezes, *whose house is across the street from ours*, are moving to San Diego.

_______ **29.** Have you been to the site *where Lincoln delivered the Gettysburg Address*?

_______ **30.** *Although we were late for the concert*, we didn't miss the first set.

C. CLASSIFYING SENTENCES ACCORDING TO STRUCTURE On the line provided, classify each sentence according to its structure. Write *S* for *simple sentence*, *CD* for *compound sentence*, *CX* for *complex sentence*, or *CD-CX* for *compound-complex sentence*.

Example _CD-CX_ **1.** Mrs. Taylor was born in March, England, and she loved to tell people that she was born in March while her birthday was actually in April.

_______ **31.** Zella and her aunt drove to the plaza, ate lunch at a Mexican restaurant, and then visited the art museum near there.

_______ **32.** The directory that was printed last week lists all the schools in the state and should therefore be a valuable resource, though it will need to be updated each year.

_______ **33.** The broken water main must be repaired immediately; otherwise, no one will have water today.

_______ **34.** The wildlife park didn't amount to much when I was a child, but now it is nationally acclaimed.

_______ **35.** The old barn near the pond on Mr. Hall's land and the dilapidated potting shed on the land next to his will soon be torn down to make room for a new public campground.

_______ **36.** According to the old saying, you can't stop progress, but I don't know why anyone would want to try to do so anyway.

_______ **37.** The first place I looked was under the porch.

_______ **38.** Few people had heard of the speaker; consequently, the event wasn't well attended.

_______ **39.** The main road was closed and the bridge was out, yet we still made it home safely and on time.

_______ **40.** The play, a comedy about people living in a small, fictional town in Texas named Tuna, opens tomorrow.

D. CLASSIFYING SENTENCES ACCORDING TO PURPOSE On the line provided, classify each sentence according to its purpose. Write *DEC* for *declarative sentence*, *IMP* for *imperative sentence*, *INT* for *interrogative sentence*, or *EXC* for *exclamatory sentence*. Then, supply the proper end mark for each sentence.

Example _IMP_ **1.** Tell me about some of the buildings of American Indians.

_______ **41.** Wow, there is such a variety of building styles

_______ **42.** Given a choice, would you rather live in a Sioux buffalo-hide tepee or a Wichita grass house

_______ **43.** Navajo hogans are still used on reservations in the Southwest

_______ **44.** Stop so that we can look at this model hogan

_______ **45.** Do you know why there were no walls in Panoan houses

_______ **46.** I wonder if all Iroquois longhouses were the same length

_______ **47.** What impressive thatch huts the Arawak designed

_______ **48.** Yahgan shelters were constructed with hides and driftwood, unless I'm mistaken

_______ **49.** Haven't you ever seen any American Indian dwellings

_______ **50.** Please draw me a picture of the Chippewa domed bark lodge that you saw

Agreement: Subject and Verb, Pronoun and Antecedent

A. IDENTIFYING VERBS THAT AGREE IN NUMBER WITH THEIR SUBJECTS   In each of the following sentences, underline the correct form of the verb in parentheses.

Example 1. The band (*enjoy*, *enjoys*) practicing on the new stadium field.

1. Either New York or Massachusetts (*top*, *tops*) Ms. Jamison's list of favorite states.

2. The myths and legends in that thick book with the dragons on the cover (*come*, *comes*) from the Chinese mainland.

3. Over two thirds of the students (*knows*, *know*) the numbers from one to fifty in Spanish.

4. Many a day here (*starts*, *start*) off cloudy but turns sunny by noon.

5. Edward Brathwaite, who was born in Bridgetown, Barbados, (*write*, *writes*) about Caribbean culture.

6. Some of the people who (*live*, *lives*) in that building will likely move if the rent goes up again.

7. Pears and cottage cheese together (*make*, *makes*) a light, tasty lunch.

8. *Chariots of Fire* (*is*, *are*) an inspiring movie about runners, isn't it?

9. Good language skills (*was*, *were*) one of the requirements for the position.

10. To launch a spacecraft from Earth and have it land where it should on Mars (*seems*, *seem*) like an astounding feat to me.

11. During dinner the family always (*share*, *shares*) stories about the day.

12. (*Don't*, *Doesn't*) the bird calls on this CD seem realistic to you?

13. (*Was*, *Were*) they discussing Margaret Atwood's poetry or her novels?

14. Melanie is active in several sports, but gymnastics (*rank*, *ranks*) as her favorite.

15. David found that no one else in any of his classes (*has*, *have*) been to as many countries as he has.

16. Here (*is*, *are*) several of the phone numbers that you asked me to copy for you.

17. Many of the adults (*have*, *has*) taken rumba lessons with an instructor from Cuba.

18. "(*Do*, *Does*) any of these articles give you the information you need, Lisa?"

19. A discussion of the Mexican American labor movement, as well as of the important figures in it, (*takes*, *take*) up half the book.

20. Either my brother or my sisters usually (*volunteers*, *volunteer*) to do the laundry.

B. IDENTIFYING ANTECEDENTS AND WRITING PRONOUNS In each of the following sentences, underline the correct pronoun in parentheses. Then, circle the antecedent of that pronoun.

Example 1. Do you know when the winter Olympics will be and where (*it, they*) will be held?

21. Mr. Ferguson startled the class by requiring (*it, them*) to write short autobiographical poems.

22. Everyone in the small group of finalists hoped (*their, his or her*) name would be called.

23. Scott is one of the seniors who may become valedictorian because of (*his, their*) high grades, especially in honors classes.

24. All of the fish in the school along the edge of the reef darted to safety when (*it, they*) saw the barracuda.

25. We have been studying genetics, and (*it, they*) is finally beginning to make sense to me.

26. Since Jennifer, Kimberly, and Carlotta might need to leave soon, (*she, they*) will have pictures taken first.

27. "You'll have to pay the five dollars because I don't have (*it, them*)," M. J. said.

28. I hope that either Danny or Ezra will let me borrow (*his, their*) in-line skates since we all wear the same size.

29. One of the women in the play had rehearsed (*her, their*) part for two months.

30. Everybody working on the trail maintenance crews usually brings (*his or her, their*) own water to drink.

C. PROOFREADING SENTENCES FOR SUBJECT-VERB AND PRONOUN-ANTECEDENT AGREEMENT Most of the following sentences contain errors in agreement. Draw a line through each incorrect verb or pronoun, and write the correct form above it. If a sentence is already correct, write *C* on the line provided.

Example ______ **1.** The summons ~~were~~ *was* served Wednesday, but I don't know who received ~~them~~ *it*.

______ **31.** Kathryn, who helped in many ways on two other political campaigns, usually are one of the first to volunteer.

______ **32.** Either Richard or Luke have already bought themselves a new jacket this fall.

______ **33.** Those scissors can be used to cut fabric, but it should not be used to cut paper.

______ **34.** Baking large, puffy Middle Eastern pitas, like the ones my mom and my grandmother make, require a very hot oven.

______ **35.** Several of the students usually are tardy because his or her bus gets to school late.

_______ **36.** Either the dog or the cats has torn the back screen.

_______ **37.** "Five thousand dollars are a good start for the fund-raiser," the chairperson said.

_______ **38.** That white-and-orange goldfish in the small bowl, in addition to the three orange ones

in the aquarium, were purchased last month.

_______ **39.** Here's the books you wanted about the art of bonsai.

_______ **40.** Each of the girls do indeed intend to offer their suggestions to the boys.

_______ **41.** The Algonquian languages, according to the dictionary, numbers more than twenty.

_______ **42.** Are any of the blackberry bushes blooming yet?

_______ **43.** The three museums in this area that has contributed artifacts for the Egyptian mummy

exhibit claim to have five hundred mummies among it.

_______ **44.** None of the apples was organic, so we decided not to eat any of it.

_______ **45.** The comedy sketches is the best part of the show, as every member of the audience

agree.

_______ **46.** Barbara and Theresa plans to bring in her science projects tomorrow.

_______ **47.** "*Dances with Wolves* make me cry every time I see it," Linda said.

_______ **48.** The Camp Fire Boys and Girls were an organization only for girls, until 1975, when

they opened admission to boys, too.

_______ **49.** Many times, the newspaper staff works long hours to meet their deadlines.

_______ **50.** The new wallpaper is nice, but it don't coordinate with the old furniture.

CHAPTER TEST

Using Pronouns Correctly: Case Forms of Pronouns; Special Pronoun Problems

A. CHOOSING CORRECT PRONOUN FORMS AND IDENTIFYING CASE Underline the correct pronoun form or forms in parentheses in each of the following sentences. Then, indicate the case of the pronoun or pronouns by writing *NOM* for *nominative*, *OBJ* for *objective*, or *POS* for *possessive*.

NOM
Example 1. When the movie was over, (*she and I*, *her and me*) went to the music store.

1. Paul and (*I, me*) would like to become sportscasters.

2. My dad's uncle Roger, a Vietnam veteran, waved to (*he and she, him and her*) and saluted.

3. Has anyone here heard (*who, whom*) won the grand prize?

4. Seeing a cow jump over the moon during the play startled (*us, we*).

5. The referee called infractions against Sandie, Karen, and me; and (*we, us*) had to sit out the rest of the quarter.

6. My cousin told me that (*him, his*) asking for a raise surprised the store manager since my cousin had been an employee only two weeks.

7. The organizers of the bake sale for the Jefferson County Volunteer Fire Department will be (*her and them, she and they*).

8. Do you know whether anyone else but (*she, her*) is going?

9. While in upstate New York, Shawn's parents bought (*he, him*) a book about the Iroquois in that area.

10. Many of my friends have already handed in their research reports, but I haven't finished (*mine, my*) yet.

11. Yes, (*me, my*) buying that paper shredder was a spur-of-the-moment decision.

12. This pair of huaraches is (*hers, her*).

13. "Come to the lake with Jorge and (*I, me*)," Ramon pleaded.

14. I didn't know (*who, whom*) I would be sitting beside at the banquet last night until I got there.

15. Only (*he and we, him and us*) know the combination to the lock on the toolshed.

16. Coach Anderson said she had some special drills for (*we, us*) goalies.

17. The parrot at the pet shop will usually talk to (*whoever, whomever*) talks to it.

18. "Please allow (*I, me*)," Mr. Rose said as he reached for the bill.

19. Although it was small, the salad bar pleased (*we, us*) because the food was fresh.

20. As soon as (*she, her*) was finished with the kite, Selma handed it to Rob.

ELEMENTS OF LANGUAGE | Sixth Course

21. (*My, Mine*) biggest concern is that the floodwaters may reach our garage door.

22. "If you want to, (*you and me, you and I*) could study together," Skip offered.

23. The Japanese family gave (*her, she*) two beautiful paper masks.

24. Do you remember (*theirs, their*) street address?

25. I think that the first runner across the finish line will be (*he, him*).

B. Proofreading Sentences for Correct Pronoun Form　Most of the following sentences contain at least one pronoun that has been used incorrectly. Draw a line through each incorrect pronoun, and write the correct form above it. If a sentence is already correct, write *C* on the line provided.

Example _______ **1.** The supervisor may lend the apprentices, Bob and ~~he~~ *him*, some tools until ~~them~~ *they* can buy their own.

_______ **26.** Jonathan chose an interesting topic for hisself: famous animals in history and literature.

_______ **27.** Mrs. Giles asked the president and vice-president, Eliza and I, to join she.

_______ **28.** Jaime and myself prefer burritos, but it's okay if you ordered we chalupas.

_______ **29.** The librarians are almost always available to give whoever needs it their help.

_______ **30.** Have you and Amy decided with who you are going to the prom?

_______ **31.** Pat said that she probably has more organizational skills than me.

_______ **32.** Whom was the man standing in front of the mosque and reading from the Koran?

_______ **33.** Frank's grandmother was making a surprise for he but was happy to show we what she was doing.

_______ **34.** Just follow Janey and I to the toy store, and we'll help you select gifts for they.

_______ **35.** Seth forgot about us working out together in the gym after school.

_______ **36.** The children, eager to learn how to read, certainly appreciate the help they've gotten from Charlie and yourself.

_______ **37.** When the guests of honor, him and her, pull up in the driveway in a few minutes, signal to we by whistling.

_______ **38.** The ones whom were there ahead of time were Pearl and me.

_______ **39.** Her boss wants to speak with theirs; I don't know what's going on.

_______ **40.** Anne told Kerry and I that Kenneth just built his own weight bench.

_______ **41.** That shift manager said that she would give they double pay to work on the Fourth of July.

_______ **42.** The good Samaritans after the accident last night were them.

_______ **43.** Who did you say plays the lead role in that movie?

_______ **44.** Remember to save some pizza for the late workers, Peter and he.

_______ **45.** We were touched by the mother and sister elephants' efforts to help the baby elephant

learn to walk and them staying with the baby and protecting it until it learned how.

_______ **46.** Can they stay at the party as long as us?

_______ **47.** Matthew and him used to be best friends in elementary school.

_______ **48.** The three earned theirselves fifty extra points by knowing the capital of Venezuela.

_______ **49.** My mother's first children were twins, Natasha and me.

_______ **50.** Do you think Trish is younger than them?

Clear Reference: Pronouns and Antecedents

A. IDENTIFYING PRONOUNS AND THEIR ANTECEDENTS In each of the following sentences, underline each pronoun, and then draw an arrow from each pronoun to its antecedent.

Example 1. The students said they watched the video about Egypt and learned much from it.

1. The narrator in the video makes her home in Cairo and wrote the script herself.

2. The video takes viewers on a tour of Egyptian cities, especially Cairo, which is the national capital.

3. Remembering his geography class, Randy correctly placed Cairo along the Nile River.

4. Randy also recalled that the Nile is the longest river in the world and that it flows from south to north.

5. Carl said, "I liked the scenes of the farmers working in their fields in the Nile delta."

6. "My favorite parts," Gina added, "were the drawings of how people lived their daily lives in ancient Egypt."

7. Although Marie knew that Egypt is in Africa, she was surprised to learn part of it is in Asia.

8. One historian whom the narrator interviewed called Egypt the "birthplace of civilization."

9. Tourists, who come to Egypt from around the world, marvel at the pyramids, the Great Sphinx, and other monuments that date back thousands of years.

10. Mrs. Miller asked Marie, "Would you like to visit Egypt and see these sights for yourself?"

B. CORRECTING AMBIGUOUS AND GENERAL PRONOUN REFERENCES On the lines provided, revise the following sentences to correct ambiguous and general pronoun references.

Example 1. We went to the restaurant and it was closed again, which disappointed us, of course.

We were disappointed, of course, when we went to the restaurant and it was closed again.

11. The photograph will go in the wedding album; it's a gift from my aunt and uncle.

12. The friendship between Rich and Elliot was strained when he broke the clock.

13. That teapot has a built-in tea strainer, but it has a crack in it.

14. The fans cheered for the ballplayers as they trotted into the stadium.

15. We asked Dad whether we can go to the game with you, and he said it was okay.

16. I had never driven a go-cart before. It was fun.

17. Granddad handed Chad the saw; then he went to work.

18. Earlier we bought tomatoes and avocados for the nachos, but now we can't find them.

19. The plumber repaired the shower this afternoon. That was great news!

20. Rhonda wore Judy's blue evening dress with her scarf that matches so well.

21. We are out of tapioca pudding, but I can make some more. It won't take long.

22. As soon as Lori and Carla decorated the bulletin board, she went to lunch.

23. Our cashier was a trainee, which is why the trip to the store took so long.

24. As a child, Jen loved to play school. This helped prepare her to become a teacher.

25. Mr. Maguire appointed William hall monitor because he is very observant.

C. CORRECTING WEAK AND INDEFINITE PRONOUN REFERENCE   On the lines provided, revise the
following sentences to correct weak and indefinite pronoun references.

Example 1. They visited the aquarium and saw many beautiful ones.

They visited the aquarium and saw many beautiful fish.

26. In that magazine it has a special buyer's guide in this issue.

      ELEMENTS OF LANGUAGE | Sixth Course

27. Sam dreaded telling the librarian that he had lost one that he had checked out.

28. Each holiday season, they have a tour of lights around the lake.

29. My sister always wants to go fishing but gets bored quickly if they aren't biting.

30. Sylvia never took a cooking class, but she became a wonderful one.

31. Prior to going to the ski resort last weekend, Ed had never tried it before.

32. In most libraries, you can find someone to answer questions.

33. Ellie wants to be a farmer even though she has never set foot on one.

34. I try not to eat too much, but sometimes it is difficult not to do.

35. On the billboard, it proclaimed "Be your best!"

36. Since Luis is a book editor, people often expect him to have written one.

37. On page eighty-five in the textbook, it says that gerunds are verbals used as nouns.

38. We went to the shoe store, but I didn't see any that I liked.

39. In Alaska they have some winter days when the sun hardly shines at all.

40. Shawn likes to write poetry, but he never shows any to anyone.

Using Verbs Correctly: Principal Parts, Tense, Voice, Mood

A. PROOFREADING SENTENCES FOR CORRECT VERB FORMS Most of the following sentences contain at least one error in the use of verbs. Draw a line through each incorrect verb form, and write the correct form above it. If a sentence is already correct, write C on the line provided.

Example _______ **1.** The owner was ~~suppose~~ *supposed* to have ~~risen~~ *raised* the rent last month, but she didn't.

_______ **1.** Although we had expected the sound, the bells startled us when they actually rung.

_______ **2.** We drove all the way across town to see the Spanish dancers, who performed here last year too.

_______ **3.** The tune-up costed us two hundred dollars, but we gladly payed it.

_______ **4.** Becky wasn't sure whether her brother meaned to leave his glasses lying on the table.

_______ **5.** "Have you forgave me for being so rude yesterday?" Prudence asked.

_______ **6.** The champion horse leaped over the fence before the other horses caught up with it.

_______ **7.** The boys brung in the grocery sacks and sat them on the kitchen floor.

_______ **8.** Leo asked to drive the new car again, but Mom said he had drove it enough.

_______ **9.** I seen you setting on the bench while you were waiting for the bus.

_______ **10.** Somebody spreaded the peanut butter on both sides of the bread, but that somebody wasn't Roger.

_______ **11.** Have you ate supper already, or are you just now setting down to eat?

_______ **12.** Helena has dreamt for years of going to Japan, and now has plans to do so.

_______ **13.** "You may stay if you wish, but the others have already went," Cody told us.

_______ **14.** Did you say that when you lived in Hawaii, you use to lay on the beach and listen to the radio?

_______ **15.** The water level may raise even higher, because more rain is forecast.

_______ **16.** It appears that José has broke the old record, but we haven't got the official time yet.

_______ **17.** Eric said that his uncle once held the state championship for carving totem poles.

_______ **18.** Dave dealed the cards for the memory game of concentration, which Mom teached us years ago.

_______ **19.** Granddad had thought that the bamboo would make a good hedge, but it growed so fast that it soon taked over the whole side of the yard.

_______ **20.** Joe drunk what was left in the cup and then threw it in the trash bin.

B. USING THE DIFFERENT TENSES OF VERBS   In each of the following sentences, change the tense of the verb to the tense indicated in brackets after the sentence. Underline the verb in the sentence, and write the new form above it.

will have been attending

Example 1. Amazingly, we had attended school thirteen years by that time. (*future perfect progressive*)

21. Our club donated many hours to the food bank by the end of the year. (*future perfect*)

22. Has Kara enrolled in the defensive driving course? (*future progressive*)

23. The guest artist agreed to draw us a charcoal sketch of our two cats. (*present perfect*)

24. Most of the students had heard about the news before the announcement. (*future*)

25. That book about African American art will interest Marvin greatly. (*past emphatic*)

26. My friends and I have gone to the pool nearly every day. (*present*)

27. Yes, the mechanic will have repaired the car by Saturday. (*past perfect*)

28. Coretta has been singing Russian ballads while playing her guitar. (*past*)

29. Dad will take two weeks of vacation in June. (*present progressive*)

30. All of us wanted to see the new Will Smith movie. (*present emphatic*)

C. PROOFREADING FOR CORRECT USES OF TENSES   Most of the following sentences contain an error in the use of tenses. Cross out each incorrect verb, and write the correct form of the verb above it. If a sentence is already correct, write *C* on the line provided.

Having been shown

Example _______ **1.** ~~Shown~~ the route earlier, Travis easily found his way to the community center.

_______ **31.** The dulcimer is one of the only stringed instruments Flora has not learned to have played yet.

_______ **32.** Holding the two trays, the waiters let us pick out the desserts that we wanted.

_______ **33.** Here are some current problems with the house: The doors stick, the floors creak, and the windows leaked.

_______ **34.** If Kelly would have studied more, he would have received a higher grade.

_______ **35.** Missing the 3:00 P.M. train, I later caught the 5:00 P.M. one.

_______ **36.** Having opened some of their presents, the children squeal with excitement.

_______ **37.** I had expected my answering machine to record my calls.

_______ **38.** Mr. Fenders gives us vegetables from his garden now; last fall he gives us fruit.

_______ **39.** I probably would not have been sick if I would have had more vitamins.

_______ **40.** Forgetting my pen this morning, I had to borrow one at school.

D. UNDERSTANDING VOICE, MOOD, AND MODALS On the line provided, write a verb that is in the mood or voice or is the kind of modal given in parentheses after the sentence.

Example 1. The editors have requested that the article ___*be rewritten*___. (*present subjunctive mood*)

41. Please _______________ the salad with beets and walnuts. (*imperative mood*)

42. The children _______________ a game with their new dreidel. (*active voice*)

43. _______________ I ask you a favor? (*modal expressing permission*)

44. The hang gliders _______________ near the grove of aspens. (*indicative mood*)

45. All of the paperwork _______________ by the officer's administrative assistant. (*passive voice*)

46. If Sondra _______________ here, she would agree with us. (*past subjunctive mood*)

47. The fall schedule _______________ on the bulletin board near the office. (*passive voice*)

48. I _______________ to plan ahead more than I do. (*modal expressing an obligation or a likelihood*)

49. Nancy suggested that the privilege _______________ to the oldest in the group. (*present subjunctive mood*)

50. Perhaps we _______________ clean out our closets and recycle items no longer wanted or needed. (*modal expressing a recommendation*)

ELEMENTS OF LANGUAGE | Sixth Course

for **CHAPTER 9** **page 272**

CHAPTER TEST

Using Modifiers Correctly: Forms and Uses of Adjectives and Adverbs; Comparison

A. **IDENTIFYING MODIFIERS AND THE WORDS THEY MODIFY**   Identify whether the italicized words, phrases, and clauses in the following sentences are used as adjectives or adverbs. On the line provided, write *ADJ* for *adjective* and *ADV* for *adverb*. Then, draw a line to the word that is modified by the italicized word or group of words.

Example ___ADV___ **1.** *In a recent magazine,* I read about the natural beauty of Latin America and the Caribbean.

_______ **1.** That area is one of the *most* biologically diverse regions in the world.

_______ **2.** In Guatemala, I'd like to see the sparkling waterfalls and lagoons in the *Cobán* rain forest.

_______ **3.** Do you think that the growers around Lake Isabel would let us wander *through their pineapple, mango, and avocado orchards*?

_______ **4.** Diving off the Bay Islands of Honduras looks especially *appealing* to me.

_______ **5.** Those *who want to see hundreds of varieties of orchids and birds* should visit Trinidad and Tobago.

_______ **6.** The first place *in the Caribbean* to be named a World Heritage site is Dominica's Trois Pitons National Park.

_______ **7.** *If you visit St. Vincent and The Grenadines,* you'll definitely want to visit beaches.

_______ **8.** The volcano on St. Vincent is more *than four thousand feet high* and is still active.

_______ **9.** You can get to many *of the natural attractions* of Costa Rica very easily.

_______ **10.** One of the *more* exciting attractions there is a cable system that offers visitors a chance to swing through a cloud forest as high as seventy feet from the forest floor.

B. **SELECTING MODIFIERS TO COMPLETE SENTENCES**   Underline the correct modifier from the pair in parentheses in each of the following sentences.

Example 1. Margaret swam (*good, well*) at the district competition.

11. The guide caught only a glimpse of the cheetah because it was running so (*fast, fastly*).

12. Jacques missed several rehearsals, so it's not surprising that he performed (*bad, badly*) in the play.

13. Their new house, much larger than the old one, is (*really, real*) close to our high school.

14. The children sat (*quiet, quietly*) in their seats and waited for the bell to ring.

15. "It makes me feel (*good, well*) that you like my painting," Olin said.

16. The tiger moved so (*slow, slowly*) that it was able to get within a few yards of its prey.

17. Everyone feels (*hopeful, hopefully*) about the situation.

18. The motorist reacted (*quick, quickly*) when the truck changed lanes.

19. Have you ever noticed how (*slow, slowly*) lizards, snakes, and other reptiles move during

cold weather?

20. Steve remained (*calm, calmly*) while waiting for the results of his driver's test.

21. This coleslaw smells (*bad, badly*); you'd better throw it away.

22. The bus driver almost always looks stern, but she's (*real, really*) nice and friendly.

23. John glanced around (*quick, quickly*) to see where his teammates were.

24. On the other side of the wall, the men were speaking quite (*loud, loudly*).

25. Several people in the office were sick last week, but they feel (*good, well*) now.

26. My two younger cousins looked (*eager, eagerly*) to go to the school carnival.

27. My brother felt (*bad, badly*) about striking out in the last inning.

28. Make sure that you fill out the form (*complete, completely*) on both sides.

29. "I'm (*real, really*) glad that the trip has been postponed," Dee confessed.

30. The cold oil is pouring out of the can very (*slow, slowly*).

C. PROOFREADING SENTENCES FOR THE CORRECT USE OF MODIFIERS Each of the following sentences
contains an error in the use of modifiers. To correct each sentence, draw a line through the error and,
where necessary, write the correction in the space above. Use a caret (ʌ) to show where any word or
words need to be added to the sentence.

Example 1. Looking at the three trees, I'd say the persimmon is the ~~most~~ healthiest.

31. The new car gets such good mileage that we can go much fartherer on a tank of gas.

32. It is warmest now that two baseboard heaters are turned on.

33. That cereal is more nutritional than any kind.

34. Your ring is more unique than any I've seen.

35. The teams are evenlier matched than they were last year.

36. Our cat often looks more happier than any of the human members of the family.

37. My brother looks for the excitingest rides he can find at carnivals.

38. After hearing the details of the plan, the supervisor was least interested in it.

CHAPTER TEST

39. Jamie's handwriting is legibler than mine is.

40. Megan lives closer to Ruth than Tamara.

41. What is the worse case of hiccups you've ever had?

42. Of the three sisters, Rachel is the more artistically inclined.

43. Mr. Cole is the popularest teacher in our school.

44. Can you tell me the name of the most longest street in your city?

45. Dwayne is the less likely student in the class to forget an assignment.

46. We liked the movie we saw last night most than the one we watched this evening.

47. Connie types more words per minute than anyone in her class.

48. The stairs in the new building are longer than any other building.

49. After spending most of the morning at the animal shelter, we decided to adopt the most little puppy that was there.

50. It's difficult to tell which of the septuplets is the most cheerfulest.

Placement of Modifiers: Misplaced and Dangling Modifiers

A. CORRECTING MISPLACED MODIFIERS   Most of the following sentences contain misplaced modifiers. On the line provided, revise each incorrect sentence so that the meaning is clear. If the sentence is already correct, write *C* on the line.

Example 1. Soaked in oil, the man threw away the rag.

The man threw away the rag soaked in oil.

1. We took our parakeet to the vet that lives in the cage on the patio.

2. Tony asked for directions from the mail carrier to his aunt's house.

3. Tell Freddie that Dad wants him to clean up his room.

4. Hurrying to get to the door, Florence tripped over the rocking chair legs.

5. My teacher has been collecting letters written by Victorians since 1990.

6. Max said after soccer practice Bill looked tired.

7. The dog ran away from its owner chasing a cat up a tree.

8. Leigh fastened the Zuni necklace around her neck that her stepmother had given her.

9. Amos said during Spanish class Pete seemed distracted and edgy.

10. My sister knew that she wanted to grow up to be a writer in kindergarten.

11. The principal said yesterday the custodian found the watch.

12. I watched most of the movies Cuba Gooding, Jr., has made over the weekend.

13. Since Dad admires Will Rogers, ask him about Rogers's American Indian background.

____

14. Each clerk needs a name badge who was hired since January.

____

15. Inform Jay when he returns Eli needs the information.

____

16. Leonora quickly poured the Brazilian coffee into the cup that had just been brewed.

____

17. We discussed the story that Edgar Allan Poe wrote about the House of Usher in English class.

____

18. During the meeting Yvonne said Walter had been defensive.

____

19. Doris said later Jane let her borrow the wrench to repair the faucet.

____

20. The Siberian husky enjoyed being in the snow, truly an outdoor dog.

____

B. CORRECTING DANGLING MODIFIERS   Most of the following sentences contain dangling modifiers. On the line provided, revise each incorrect sentence so that the meaning is clear. If the sentence is already correct, write C on the line.

Example 1. While waiting at the bus stop, the neon sign across the street fascinated me.

While waiting at the bus stop, I was fascinated by the neon sign across the street.

21. Snowing, the hikers wore heavy coats and caps.

____

22. Approaching the Navajo reservation, the neighboring mountain range came into view.

____

23. To solve this problem, your expertise will be crucial.

____

24. Overdrawn at the bank, Sal's finances were in disarray.

____

25. Looking through the catalog, the dresses were the prettiest Alicia had ever seen.

____

26. After becoming concerned about air pollution, Doug began walking or bicycling everywhere.

27. While hanging the clothes on the line, the wind began to blow even harder.

28. Having dusted the entire house, Barry's weekly chores were finished.

29. To make this trip, new luggage is needed.

30. In the dim early morning light, we could barely read the house numbers.

31. Sitting on the floor reading, the cat stretched out beside her.

32. Having cut her brothers' and sisters' hair for years, Jerry had become a good stylist.

33. Running around the building, the bushes nearly blocked her way.

34. Having greeted so many guests, my fingers ached from shaking hands with them all.

35. While checking the transmission fluid, the hood refused to stay up.

36. To land that job, Vivian had to pass a skills test and go to four interviews.

37. Getting out the can opener and the can of dog food, the dog's ears perked up.

38. Cloudy, the top of the tower seemed to have completely disappeared.

39. Surprised by the sudden noise, the plate fell off my lap.

40. While watching for her mother, the bus left without Shawna.

A Glossary of Usage: Common Usage Problems

A. IDENTIFYING CORRECT USAGE   In the following sentences, underline the words or expressions in parentheses that are correct according to formal, standard English.

Example 1. Our new neighbors (*emigrated, immigrated*) from Cambodia and quickly (*adapted, adopted*) the United States as their home.

1. Mr. Fowler, (*who, which*) is my dad's boss, and his wife are (*supposed to, suppose to*) come for dinner tomorrow night.

2. (*Credible, Creditable*) sources tell (*me, myself*) that old computer parts can be recycled into filler for potholes in roads.

3. The lunch bell is (*liable, likely*) to ring any minute, and I (*insure, assure*) you that I am ready!

4. "I feel (*somewhat, kind of*) rushed with (*this, this here*) deadline," Jim said to his editor.

5. Alan and my brother, both of whom are (*alumni, alumnae*) of Harvard, told me (*a lot, much*) about the university's Oriental library.

6. What (*affect, effect*), if any, did the new plant food have on (*your, you're*) azaleas?

7. Mr. Sosa (*learned, taught*) me nearly everything (*that, what*) I know about electrical work.

8. Do you think the (*amount, number*) of people who come to the party will be (*anywhere, anywheres*) close to how many we invited?

9. "(*Leave, Let*) me tell you about the most amazing (*phenomena, phenomenon*) called the Hawthorne effect!" Hal said excitedly.

10. (*Try and, Try to*) find a copy of the book (*because, being as*) it includes a great photograph of Martin Luther King, Dr. Martin Luther King, Jr., and Martin Luther King III together.

11. "We're having (*a, an*) unusually mild winter this year," the farmer observed.

12. The bully (*persecuted, prosecuted*) many new students with his actions, and a number of them (*has, have*) complained.

13. "You are behaving (*like, as though*) you are upset with me," Kendra said.

14. Will you (*borrow, lend*) me your copy of *Popol Vunh: A Sacred Book of the Maya*, and may I (*bring, take*) it now?

15. After (*a while, awhile*), perhaps fifty years or so, there will be significantly (*fewer, less*) traces of the chemical in the soil.

16. "Stacy is more observant (*than, then*) Tasha," (*their, they're*) mother noted.

17. Creative works of these (*sort, sorts*) frequently contain (*allusions, illusions*) to ancient Greece and Rome.

18. The balloon in which Bertrand Piccard and Brian Jones made their (*famous, notorious*) flight was as tall as the Leaning Tower of Pisa.

19. If you ask me, the (*amount, number*) of hours of work required for this project is too great (*anyway, anyways*).

20. The data (*show, shows*) a shift in consumer spending, and the direction of that shift (*implies, infers*) that on-line shopping will increase.

21. (*Don't, Doesn't*) you know that the Chinese New Year always occurs (*between, among*) January 21 and February 19?

22. Exercising soon after eating often makes me (*nauseated, nauseous*), so now I wait (*awhile, a while*) before working out.

23. Neither Ozzie (*or, nor*) Dallas has decided yet whether to (*accept, except*) the college's offer.

24. Yes, the merger did (*affect, effect*) the morale of the employees (*some, somewhat*).

25. After the boy ran (*in, into*) the waiting room from outside, he stopped and stood (*beside, besides*) the receptionist's desk and looked around the room.

B. PROOFREADING FOR CORRECT USAGE Most of the following sentences contain errors in the use of formal, standard English. Draw a line through each error, and where necessary, write the correct word or words above the error. Also replace any gender-specific terms with nonsexist ones. If the sentence is already correct, write C on the line provided.

                    mail carrier   *implied*

Example _______ **1.** The ~~mailman~~ yesterday ~~inferred~~ that we need a larger mailbox.

_______ **26.** Nine hundred miles in one day was all the farther we could go; we were so tired that we didn't even know where we had stopped at to get a room that night.

_______ **27.** Some people have traveled a long ways to see a live performance by the Estonian Philharmonic Chamber Choir.

_______ **28.** Hopefully, these storms ain't going to last all weekend.

_______ **29.** Timothy could of used more manpower when he was planting those trees.

_______ **30.** The credulous audience believed that the magician's allusions were real.

_______ **31.** When I'm in a hurry to write a note to myself, any type of pen or pencil will do.

_______ **32.** A maniple is when an ancient Roman legion is subdivided into 60 or 120 men.

_______ **33.** The family they watched as the rescue proceeded.

_______ **34.** The police received valuable information off of the witness and busted the intruder.

_______ **35.** My grandfather built the porch hisself, using tools his friends had lent him.

_______ **36.** The reason it will be alright if she assists is because she is a registered nurse.

_______ **37.** The largest feathered dinosaur what has ever been invented is being studied at an

institute in Beijing.

_______ **38.** We chose from between dozens of games for Jake's present.

_______ **39.** Dad told us to stay off of the porch because the paint is drying so slow.

_______ **40.** The Reverend Cynthia Diamond ensured that the congregation understood the

concept.

_______ **41.** Trudy finished early and said, "I done all my work today."

_______ **42.** You had ought to know who discovered the telephone.

_______ **43.** We asked the flight attendant to leave us have some more of them peanuts.

_______ **44.** My neighbor asked if she could borrow some plant food off my mom.

_______ **45.** Mrs. Clark, who is my journalism teacher, she said that March 16 is the anniversary

of the first African American newspaper, which was founded in 1827.

_______ **46.** We didn't scarcely have no hot water after the pipe froze and busted.

_______ **47.** The store carries mainly standard vegetables: lettuce, squash, onions, potatoes, and etc.

_______ **48.** Megan don't have but only one album by that new jazz combo.

_______ **49.** This here short story by Stephen King was adopted into a movie.

_______ **50.** What kind of a bird is that setting on the telephone wire?

Capitalization: Standard Uses of Capital Letters

A. CORRECTING ERRORS IN CAPITALIZATION Each of the following items contains at least one error in capitalization. Correct each error either by changing a capital letter to a lowercase letter or by changing a lowercase letter to a capital letter.

Example 1. the Capital of california

1. the corner of Seventy-First Street and Madison Avenue

2. aboard the Space Shuttle *Endeavour*

3. taking classes at Navajo community college

4. along the shore of the sea of Galilee

5. a winner of the Spingarn medal

6. observe the Jewish Holiday Passover

7. a town in Northeastern Illinois

8. the house of Representatives

9. Art, Economics, and Chemistry II

10. works at Ames-Dryden flight research center

11. Hear us, o minerva.

12. Memorial day weekend vacation

13. Yours Truly, Mr. Alberto t. Santiago, jr.

14. owns a Kenmore® Refrigerator

15. a performance at the Globe theatre

16. written by Author Tomás Rivera

17. the movie *Voyage To The Bottom Of The Sea*

18. my Great-aunt Mae from san Francisco

19. a long hike in Grand Canyon national park

20. The teacher said, "sit still."

21. Resolved: that every child in the United States should start each school day with a nutritious meal.

22. fought in the Battle of Mobile bay

23. atop the Empire state building

24. a Bank in Dade city

25. Mercury, Venus, earth, and mars

B. CORRECTING CAPITALIZATION ERRORS IN SENTENCES   Each of the following sentences contains at least one error in capitalization. Correct each error by changing a capital letter to a lowercase letter or by changing a lowercase letter to a capital letter.

Example 1. Our School Library subscribes to both newspapers with the largest circulation in new Mexico: the *Albuquerque Journal* and the *Albuquerque Tribune*.

26. In *Self-Portrait With Thorn Necklace and Hummingbird*, painter Frida Kahlo alludes to an ancient practice of Aztec Priests.

27. My Cousin Samuel has been accepted at the United States air force academy and is looking forward to serving as an officer.

28. We named our new chow puppy Iditarod (ditz, for short), after the Iditarod Trail Sled Dog Race held in alaska each march.

29. While we were in Northwestern Minnesota last summer, we visited lake Itasca, the source of the Mississippi river.

30. Among the many rock musicians influenced by blues great Muddy Waters were Mick Jagger, the Vocalist of the Rolling stones, and Elvis Presley.

31. The garage sale at the Lions club included the following items: Clothing, toys, books, and household appliances.

32. Marcia asked, "did anyone happen to notice where I left my new Parker™ Pen?"

33. Bob replied, "I think I saw it on the file cabinet in the Principal's office."

34. The Librarian at the Kane County public library recommended William Loren Katz's book *Black Indians: a Hidden Heritage*.

35. The question is, how can we persuade more students to attend our upcoming Junior-senior Follies?

36. Elected Governor of Washington in 1996, Gary Locke became the first Chinese american chief executive of a state in this country.

37. During a solar eclipse, the moon moves between the Earth and the sun.

38. My favorite exhibit at the National Air and Space museum is the *Spirit Of St. Louis*, the airplane in which Charles A. Lindbergh flew from New York city to Paris in 1927.

39. Are we supposed to answer all the study questions at the end of the next chapter, "national politics and culture, 1867–1869," in *The Story of America*?

40. Last Summer my family rented a cabin in Linville, north Carolina, near Grandfather mountain.

41. The island nation of Singapore is located just off the Southern coast of the Malay Peninsula, near where the south China Sea and the Indian Ocean converge.

42. Among the many awards the Late Mother Teresa won during her lifetime was the Jawaharlal Nehru award for International Understanding.

43. The Monterey pine, which is native to California, has become a valuable source of timber in several countries in the southern hemisphere, including Chile, new Zealand, and South Africa.

44. Before being named Secretary of State in 1997, Madeleine Albright was a Professor at Georgetown University and United States ambassador to the united Nations.

45. Opened in 1995, the Rock and roll Hall of Fame and Museum in Cleveland, ohio, was designed by Architect I. m. Pei.

46. Pieces of pottery found in Arizona's Petrified Forest national park suggest that American Indians may have lived in the area as early as A.D. 500.

47. At our family reunion great-aunt Leonora told me about her experiences as an Aide to a member of the Senate during the Gulf War.

48. The March of Dimes Birth Defects foundation grew out of the national Foundation for Infantile Paralysis, which president Franklin D. Roosevelt established in 1938 to fight Polio.

49. I got a great deal on a new cd player at the soundsabound Store in the Westside mall.

50. After she became deputy Postmaster of Seneca falls, N.Y., in 1849, Amelia Jenks Bloomer declared that her aim was to provide "A practical demonstration of woman's right to fill any place for which she had capacity."

Punctuation: End Marks and Commas

A. USING END MARKS AND COMMAS CORRECTLY   The following sentences lack necessary end marks and commas. Insert the correct punctuation in each sentence.

Example 1. Andrew, would you like one of these sweet, juicy oranges?

1. Wild rice a food source high in vitamins and proteins is grown commercially in Wisconsin and Minnesota

2. Actually wild rice is a grass I believe

3. Well whatever it is it certainly is delicious

4. With her April 1993 journey aboard the space shuttle *Discovery* Ellen Ochoa became the first Hispanic woman in space

5. Dad exclaimed, "What a mess the traffic was tonight"

6. Strawberries and bananas and cantaloupe were just three of the healthful appealing selections on the lavish breakfast buffet

7. As a matter of fact it was Luis not Frank who came up with the idea for the skit

8. The meeting has been rescheduled for several of the committee members had other commitments

9. Lani wants to know which of the Wright brothers piloted the first flight on that historic day December 17 1903

10. Elated I called Mom at work to tell her about the letter of acceptance I had just received from Bethune-Cookman College

11. The assembly honoring the students who have served on Teen Court this year will be held at 2:00 P M on Friday May 7

12. Our speaker today students is Ms Erica B Robinson PhD whose talents and determination have taken her a long way since her days here at Edgewater High School

13. Puzzled by the idiom "straight from the horse's mouth," Chim asked, "What does a horse have to do with anything"

14. The issue of course may not be as easy to resolve as we had thought it would be

15. Oh how I wish I could go swimming with you this afternoon

16. The eerie mournful wail of the bagpipes stirred the listeners deeply and many shed a tear

17. "Before you leave Lee will you help me move the boxes that are in the family room into the garage" I asked

18. Brandon expecting a call from his friend April stayed close to the telephone

19. For her niece Sue Ellen bought a dreidel a top used in a game popular during Hanukkah

20. This package which was delivered to our house by mistake is addressed to Prof Helen K

Andreas 17 N Prospector St Chicago IL 60610

21. The photographer posed the family adjusted the lighting and shot several pictures

22. After we have finished washing the windows let's make a pitcher of lemonade and sit on the

porch for a while

23. Anyone interested in joining the Ecology Club's field trip on Saturday to the Great Dismal

Swamp should sign up in the office by Friday

24. The teacher asked Mary what year Zanzibar and Tanganyika united to form Tanzania

25. Mary asked, "Could you repeat the question"

B. **PROOFREADING SENTENCES FOR THE CORRECT USE OF END MARKS AND COMMAS** Proofread the
following sentences and the final short item, adding or deleting periods, question marks, exclamation
points, and commas as necessary. If a sentence is already correct, write *C* on the line provided.

Example _______ **1.** I like your idea/for a fund-raiser,Ramon,but I think the club should

vote on it.

_______ **26.** Let's pack a picnic, and ride our bikes to the park?

_______ **27.** While she and her family were in hiding, from the Nazis Anne Frank kept an intimate

moving diary of her thoughts and experiences.

_______ **28.** I could tell, by the way, you spoke that you feel strongly about the matter.

_______ **29.** The League of Women Voters which welcomes both men and women to become mem-

bers encourages people to become educated, involved citizens.

_______ **30.** Formed in 1920 the league grew out of the movement, to win the right for women to

vote.

_______ **31.** That voting is one of the most important rights citizens of this nation have, is undeni-

ably true.

_______ **32.** Incidentally if you haven't registered to vote yet, the supervisor of elections will have a

voter-registration booth at the mall this weekend

_______ **33.** Yes, Majid eighteen is the minimum voting age, in the United States.

______ **34.** Rising 630 feet above the city of St. Louis the Gateway Arch, designed by Eero Saarinen was completed in 1965.

______ **35.** Hey, Look out for that truck

______ **36.** Aunt Ann asked me if we are going to be home this weekend?

______ **37.** Martin Luther King, III, president of the King Center for Nonviolent Social Change (KCNSC) was one of the speakers, who addressed the crowd.

______ **38.** With the barbecued chicken we served coleslaw, freshly picked corn on the cob, and homemade, buttermilk biscuits.

______ **39.** Having unplugged the answering machine to change the battery, I guess I forgot to plug it in again.

______ **40.** My first dog Duchess, was a boxer a sturdy, medium-sized dog related to the bulldog.

______ **41.** Mom, a Mr Alfonzo P Snodgrass has sent you an invitation to a seminar

______ **42.** Are you as tired as I am of hearing the expression, "Have a nice day?"

______ **43.** The people, who say that, mean well I suppose, but it certainly can be tiresome I admit.

______ **44.** As we came out of the theater we saw Dr Hightower our dentist, and her husband Jack

______ **45.** Would you please call me, when you reach a decision

______ **46.** After all, this time it's hard to believe construction on that road still isn't finished.

______ **47.** Handwriting on silk, was considered an art form in China as early as the fifth century BC.

______ **48.** Astronaut, Shannon Lucid earned her PhD. in biochemistry from the University of Oklahoma.

______ **49.** The time you spend revising your paper, and the time you spend proofreading it are valuable investments in a good grade not a waste of effort.

______ **50.** Dear Elena

Here's the card, that I promised you. San Francisco is stunning I'll tell you all about my trip when I get home.

Love

Dad

Punctuation: Other Marks of Punctuation

A. CORRECTING SENTENCES BY ADDING SEMICOLONS AND COLONS Each of the following sentences is missing at least one semicolon or colon. Correct each sentence by inserting the missing punctuation mark. Use a caret ($_\wedge$) to show where each semicolon or colon should go.

Example 1. Father's flight departs at 645 A.M. therefore, he will finish packing tonight and go to bed earlier than he usually does.

1. Radios, electronic games, and earphones are forbidden on the camp-out however, you will need the following items a sleeping bag, a flashlight, a canteen, towels, toiletries, and warm clothing.

2. *Guns, Germs, and Steel The Fates of Human Societies* by Jared Diamond provides a fascinating view on how the modern world was formed.

3. Jacob will read aloud to the class Genesis 6 5–8 I will read aloud Revelation 14 1–3.

4. The band's members represent various American cultures The drummer is from Lima, Peru the lead guitarist is from Mexico City, Mexico the bass guitarist is from Denver, Colorado and the singer is from Calgary, Canada.

5. Please find a seat as soon as the 9 15 bell rings the test will begin at that time.

6. Sir Arthur Conan Doyle is probably best remembered for his Sherlock Holmes stories, such as *The Sign of Four, The Hound of the Baskervilles,* and *His Last Bow* but, according to Mrs. Jones, his historical romances are equally good.

7. The 1993 inaugural address of United States President William J. Clinton begins with these words "My fellow citizens, today we celebrate the mystery of American renewal. This ceremony is held in the depth of winter, but by the words we speak and the faces we show the world, we force the spring."

8. Although the official language of Costa Rica is Spanish, the following languages are also spoken English, a Creole form of English, and the indigenous Bribri.

9. Given her choice, Mother prefers listening to the album *Invocations Sacred Music from World Traditions* however, the rest of our family likes jazz.

10. Mara painted her sculpture three vibrant colors She painted the head and neck orange, the trunk lime green, and the appendages purple.

B. CORRECTING SENTENCES BY ADDING UNDERLINING, QUOTATION MARKS, OTHER PUNCTUATION MARKS, AND CAPITALIZATION   In the following sentences, insert underlining, quotation marks, and other marks of punctuation where they are needed. Use a caret ($\wedge$) to show where each punctuation mark should go. Circle any lowercase letters that should be capitalized.

Example 1. My peer editor advised, remove several *ands* to shorten the sentences in this paragraph.

11. My family's favorite movie is The Sound of Music said Lola. my sister knows all the songs.

12. Miss Tays inquired has anyone in the class read Doris Lessing's short story titled No Witchcraft for Sale

13. Repeating uh throughout your speech, explained the speech teacher detracts from your message.

14. Have you seen Brian Forbes's painting called The Olympic Runner asked Rosita.

15. How excited our puppy gets whenever one of the family members says let's go for a walk

16. As the result of a national competition involving students at all grade levels, President George H. W. Bush announced in 1989 that the new Space Shuttle would be named Endeavour.

17. I can't believe that Lewis Carroll, the author of Alice's Adventures in Wonderland, is not responsible for the phrase mad as a hatter exclaimed Tessa.

18. The first chapter of Annie Dillard's book Pilgrim at Tinker Creek is entitled Heaven and Earth in Jest said Mrs. Ritacco please read the chapter for homework tonight.

19. The Sioux generally call themselves Lakota or Dakota, meaning allies.

20. Amy said when my brother gets home from school, the first thing he says is what's for dinner

C. CORRECTING SENTENCES BY ADDING APOSTROPHES   Insert apostrophes where they are needed in the following sentences. Use a caret to show where each apostrophe goes.

Example 1. Arent Kims and Erics semester grades all As?

21. Jorges, Rachels, and my project cant be turned in until tomorrow.

22. After an hours wait, the surveillance team saw Mr. Browns and the police officers cars pull up to the house simultaneously.

23. My best friends sister wont be able to attend tonights concert with us.

24. By two oclock the jury had heard the M. D.s report and both witnesses testimonies.

25. Ive noticed that the children's *e*s look like *i*s.

26. I wasnt sure whether the books and backpack were hers or yours, so I put them in the schools lost-and-found box.

27. Fathers employees commented that after a weeks vacation everyones morale is boosted.

28. According to that opinion poll, the 70s was almost no ones favorite decade.

29. Didnt Ms. Flynn base her screenplay on one Ph. D.s notes and several womens memoirs?

30. Lets give that little girls mother a few minutes rest.

D. Correcting Sentences by Adding Hyphens, Dashes, Parentheses, and Brackets Insert hyphens, dashes, parentheses, and brackets where they are needed in the following sentences. Use a caret (∧) to show where each punctuation mark goes. Circle any lowercase letters that should be capitalized.

Example 1. Grand Cayman a world famous vacation spot is an island that lies northwest of Jamaica. See the map on page 872.

31. Did the governor elect I can't recall his name receive two thirds of our precinct's votes?

32. The total area of western Africa's Senegal see the chart on page 56 Diagram C is 196,722 sq km about 75,954 sq mi .

33. Coach Moore exclaimed, "Let me reemphasize what is most important in tonight's game winning!"

34. The MidAtlantic Ridge, which is approximately 15,000 kilometers about 9300 miles long, breaks the ocean's surface to form seven islands and groups of islands Iceland, the Azores, Saint Peter and Saint Paul Rocks, Ascension, Saint Helena, Tristan da Cunha, and Bouvet.

35. According to a well informed source, fifty three applicants are vying for the job.

36. Our nearly finished project you probably already know this was damaged by last night's rain.

37. The owner of that craft shop The Snippy Scissors claims that recovering a chair with velvet is easy.

38. The article quoted Principal Rodrigues as saying, "We are proud of our school, its faculty, and its students. It our school has been the launching pad for twenty one classes of seniors."

39. All sugar free and fat free foods have been relocated to the newly constructed section for health products. are they really considered health foods?

40. A well known celebrity bragged, "After the release of my first movie in 1998 sic, fame was inevitable."

Spelling: Improving Your Spelling

A. PROOFREADING SENTENCES TO CORRECT MISSPELLED WORDS AND ERRORS IN THE USE OF NUMBERS

In the following sentences, draw a line through each misspelled word and each number that has been written incorrectly. Write the correction above the word or number you have crossed out.

Example 1. I ~~mispelled~~ *misspelled* Jamaica; it has ~~3 as.~~ *three a's*

1. Many couragous soldeirs have risked thier lives for thier homelands.

2. Our coachs have introduced a sensible exercise program to increase our strength, flexibility, and leaness.

3. Several veterans of the Foreign Legion and their wifes attendded the celebration.

4. Both of my sister-in-laws are alumnaes of Fairmont State College.

5. The photographers' lifelike decoies fooled the unsuspecting wild gooses.

6. Aunt Kim scolded, "Ignoring your household responsibilitys is unnacceptable."

7. Before proceding, be sure the childs fasten their seat belts.

8. The store manager permited delivery of only 10 50-pound bags of concrete.

9. Our allys finaly succeded in penetrateing enemy lines.

10. My salsa recipe includes tomatos, onions, pepperes, and several secret ingredients.

11. 4 of the removeable cieling panels are damaged and must be replaced.

12. Both editor-in-chiefs offerred Julio summer emploiment.

13. Placeing 5th in the race is quite an accomplishment, considering the competition.

14. Although our politicses are disimilar, our friendship is strong.

15. Unfortunatly, both radioes need new batterys, which are unavailable at this store.

16. Can happyness truly be acheived through material gain?

17. Please add 2 heaping tablespoonsful of flour to the dough.

18. Are the Chineses seriously affected by the recent trade embargos?

19. Her recent family crisises have not robed Sara of her sense of humor.

20. The vacant lot is littered with piles of trash, leafs, and branchs.

21. For some unexplained reason, most of the *es* in this document are blured.

22. All of the sopranos and two of the altoes sang their soloes a cappella.

23. I think we'd better turn down the volume on those music videoes before the neighbors become annoied and complain.

24. Queen Elizabeth II's riegn over the United Kingdom and the Commonwealth began in nineteen hundred fifty-three.

25. The frieght train from Pittsburgh arrives dayly at 2 o'clock.

B. **DISTINGUISHING BETWEEN WORDS OFTEN CONFUSED**   Underline the correct word in each set of parentheses in the following sentences.

> **Example 1.** (*Their, They're*) using cotton (*clothes, cloths*) for dusting.

26. I have (*all ready, already*) determined the (*moral, morale*) of this story.

27. Our tour guide, dressed in a (*plain, plane*) navy blue suit, greeted us on the steps of the (*capital, capitol*).

28. In (*their, they're*) quest for safety, the refugees have (*born, borne*) many hardships.

29. (*All right, Alright*), you may have the honor of inserting the last puzzle (*peace, piece*).

30. When the (*principal, principle*) was absent, who (*lead, led*) the school song?

31. (*All together, Altogether*), the city (*council, counsel*) have decided to ratify the proposal to build a light rail system.

32. Did the Indian Civil Rights Act of 1968 (*assure, insure*) Native American tribes that ancestral lands would be restored (*to, too, two*) them?

33. Aunt Sita helped me (*choose, chose*) accessories to (*complement, compliment*) my new outfit.

34. I use monogrammed (*stationary, stationery*) for my (*personal, personnel*) correspondence.

35. The camp (*councilor, counselor*) made sure that the boys were (*all ready, already*) for the hike.

36. I (*assure, ensure*) you that I will not (*waist, waste*) your time or your money.

37. Our state's new governor was (*formally, formerly*) a coal (*miner, minor*) and a schoolteacher.

38. I cautiously applied the (*brake, break*) as the car (*passed, past*) on my left.

39. If we slightly (*altar, alter*) our (*coarse, course*), we can visit the National Museum of African Art.

40. The (*plain, plane*) does not arrive until (*later, latter*) this afternoon.

41. When (*its, it's*) raining, I look for a (*quiet, quite*), secluded place to read.

42. You can (*brake, break*) that old pocket watch by winding it (*to, too, two*) tightly.

43. Given the choice of raising more (*capital, capitol*) or cutting back on our plans, we choose the (*later, latter*).

44. Is (*their, there*) a (*stationary, stationery*) bicycle or a treadmill in the weight room?

45. "(*Your, You're*) taller (*than, then*) I am!" exclaimed Nathan incredulously.

46. (*Who's, Whose*) the company's director of (*personal, personnel*)?

47. Characterized by (*its, it's*) black lava formations and hot springs, Ethiopia's Denakil (*Desert, Dessert*) is one of the hottest places on earth.

48. Never (*loose, lose*) sight of (*your, you're*) goals.

49. The promise of (*peace, piece*) boosted the refugees' (*moral, morale*).

50. Do you prefer a (*loose, lose*), flowing dress or one that is belted at the (*waist, waste*)?

Correcting Common Errors

A. CORRECTING SENTENCE FRAGMENTS AND RUN-ON SENTENCES   On the line provided, identify each word group below as a sentence fragment, a run-on sentence, or a complete sentence. Write *F* for fragment, *R* for run-on, or *S* for a complete sentence. If a word group is a fragment or a run-on sentence, add, change, or delete words or punctuation to make it a complete sentence. Capitalization may also need to be changed.

Example ____*R*___ **1.** Ramon is saving for college ⊙*H* ̸he saves half of his paycheck each week.

______ **1.** Because my car can accommodate only four passengers and their luggage.

______ **2.** In 1991, South African writer Nadine Gordimer won the Nobel Prize for literature her first story was published when she was fifteen years old.

______ **3.** Operated by wires above the stage, the marionettes whose features seemed lifelike.

______ **4.** To become a knight was all that the squire desired to achieve his goal took many years.

______ **5.** The walls of the pharaohs' tombs were adorned with paintings, most of which portrayed mythological subjects and scenes from everyday life.

B. CORRECTING ERRORS IN USAGE   Each of the following sentences contains at least one error in usage. Correct each error by adding or deleting a word or words. Capitalization and punctuation may also need to be changed.

Example 1. ~~Neither~~ *That neither* of the salads ~~were~~ *was* fresh, ~~which~~ made Mother angry.

6. Competing against everyone on the track team, Alex has consistently ran the fastest; however, he doesn't never brag about his victories.

7. "The reason I feel like I might faint is because this room is hot," Ginny told Lisa and I.

8. Before it gets broke, please sit that vase back a little ways further on the counter.

9. Since the volunteers at Meals on Wheels can't hardly make all their deliveries, one of we seniors need to volunteer to help.

10. In this article it don't fully explain how the Rails-to-Trails Conservancy originated.

11. Just between you and I, my dad and sister and me are secretly designing a new kitchen for Mother, but it is taking longer than we planned.

12. Although we hadn't sang together in weeks, Rita and me performed surprisingly good in last night's talent show.

13. I implied from Martha's e-mail message that she is taking less classes this semester.

14. "Who knocked that platter off of the table and busted it?" asked Chip in his innocentest voice.

15. Both of the men told Jill and myself that he has swam in the river and that it ain't too cold,

but it felt awful chilly to us.

C. REVISING SENTENCES TO CORRECT MISPLACED AND DANGLING MODIFIERS On the line provided, revise each sentence to correct the misplaced or dangling modifier.

Example 1. To complete your research project on time, a schedule is necessary.

To complete your research project on time, you need a schedule.

16. Students at that boarding school only go home during major holidays.

____

17. I finished reading Daniel Yergin's book that won the Pulitzer Prize during spring break.

____

18. When lifting weights, a spotter should always be used for safety.

____

19. There is a large bird at our bird feeder that has unusually colorful feathers.

____

20. Dana approached the finish line triumphantly waving to the spectators.

____

D. CORRECTING SENTENCES BY ADDING CAPITALIZATION AND PUNCTUATION Each of the following sentences contains at least one error in the use of capitalization, punctuation, or italics. Circle each lowercase letter that should be capitalized, and insert each punctuation mark that is needed. Underline any word or letter that should be italicized. Use a caret ($_\wedge$) to show where you insert a hyphen or a dash.

Example 1. "how many u̲s̲ are in uruguay? asked Sam, who rarely needs help with spelling.

21. Although we have only one remaining week of our European vacation we still hope to visit

the following cities marseilles, france barcelona, spain and lisbon, portugal.

22. at 7 00 P.M. Itzhak Perlman a world renowned violinist will perform at bass concert hall

23. Our schools theater arts department has scheduled a performance of A Doll's House by the

norwegian playwright Henrik Ibsen 1826–1906.

24. At last nights political rally senator gibson and her opponent I cant remember his name

participated in a forty five minute debate.

25. I cant believe we won exclaimed Marta With only two seconds left in the game Carlos made an unbelievable three point shot

26. Mothers grocery list includes bread milk kidney beans apples and carrots.

27. Mrs Sharpe who supervises the local branch of the living well insurance agency encouraged me to get an m.d.s referral.

28. Your reading assignment said miss Goethel is Graham Greene's short story The Destructors.

29. Yes I see all the ys look like vs in this letter my printer obviously needs a new ink cartridge.

30. The eastern Indian city of calcutta see the map on page 168 Diagram B inspired a number of films by director Mrinal Sen my favorite is Calcutta, '71.

31. Turning to her mother Aretha asked did the conductor say All passengers please find a seat

32. At aunt Irenes house her five dogs fourteen cats and four birds create chaos consequently my aunt has few visitors.

33. Im sure coach Ivy will give you some antiinflammatory ointment for your ankle said Claire.

34. I wasn't sure if the book titled where the sidewalk ends was yours or the childrens so i left it in the car.

35. Did you know that the word hippopotamus is derived from the Greek words hippos meaning horse and potamos meaning river asked Franz.

E. PROOFREADING SENTENCES TO CORRECT MISSPELLED WORDS AND ERRORS IN THE USE OF NUMBERS In the following sentences, cross out any misspelled word or any number that has been written incorrectly, and above it, write the correct word or number.

Example 1. ~~Whose~~ *Who's* responsible for ~~houseing~~ *housing* the ~~22 chief of staffs~~ *twenty-two chiefs of staff*?

36. Many people are recycling more of they're waist then they used to in the past.

37. I ensure you that this restaurant's food is definitly overated; the 1st time I ate here, the peace of turkey I had was overcooked, and now my potatos are undercooked.

38. Of coarse, having to forfiet the game was a dissappointment, for our team has exceled this season and won 19 of the 21 games we've played.

39. Neither officer knows the principle cause of the accident, so the authoritys will procede with an investigation.

40. Wearing lose, light-colored cloths provides some relief from the intense heat and driness in dessert areas.

Writing Clear Sentences

COORDINATING AND SUBORDINATING IDEAS

DIRECTIONS Complete each of the following sentences by deciding which connecting words or subordinating conjunctions will best fit in the blank. Remember to use the correct punctuation as necessary. Use the headings above each set of sentences to guide you.

Example A bicycle has two wheels ____, *but*____ a unicycle has only one.

Using Appropriate Connectives

1. Spring was still a few weeks away ________ the plants were beginning to flower.

2. Mrs. Smith might teach ________ French ________ Spanish next year.

3. ________ Sandy ________ Charlie decided to try out for the debate team last week.

4. You need to chew your food ________ you might choke on it.

Choosing Appropriate Subordinating Conjunctions

5. ________ we could leave on our trip, we had to take the dog to the kennel.

6. Many new administrators are learning about project management ________ they can make better scheduling plans.

7. ________ many people make higher wages than they did five years ago, it seems that they have less money to spend.

ACHIEVING CLARITY

DIRECTIONS Revise each of the following items. Remember to use the correct punctuation as necessary. Use the headings above each set of sentences to guide you. Make your corrections between the lines.

Example   *Although* ̸Contributions from many local businesses were made to the representative's campaign. He failed to win in the primary.

Inserting Adverb Clauses

8. Students crowded onto the field. The coaches finally announced the schedule for the tryouts.

9. Sharla is in bed with the flu. Sharla will have to drink plenty of water.

10. You should eat fruits and vegetables. They are good for you.

Correcting Faulty Coordination

11. Kayla did well at the speech contest and she is very shy.

12. The bus was at the end of the street and was waiting for the last students.

Correcting Faulty Parallelism

13. In the summer I really enjoy swimming laps and to play basketball.

14. The corporation guaranteed the employees medical benefits and that they would get extra

pay for overtime.

Eliminating Fragments and Run-ons

15. My baby brother constructs towers of blocks. And knocks them down.

16. The judges thought. That the second team had done exceedingly well at all aspects of the

tournament.

17. The autumn wind briskly moved through the trees crisp leaves fell like confetti on top of the

parade of cars heading into the city.

Eliminating Unnecessary Shifts in Subject, Tense, and Voice

18. She wanted to register for the night class but mistakenly registers for the day class instead.

19. The committee members discussed various changes to be made to the charter, but no final

vote was taken.

20. All team members need to be present at the practice so that you can participate in the

competition.

REVISING A PASSAGE

DIRECTIONS The following paragraphs need to be revised. Make your revisions in the space between the lines. Use what you have learned to improve the paragraph in the following ways:

- Choose appropriate subordinating conjunctions
- Correct faulty parallelism
- Eliminate fragments and run-ons
- Eliminate unnecessary shifts in voice

The Shopping Assignment

Ms. Salvatore gave her economics students a shopping assignment. They were to look for bargains. She gave each student a list of four items to find: a hair fastener, a musical item, something made of metal, and something made of cotton.

The students were not expected to spend any money. Instead, they were to fill out a form. **(21)** They had to describe the item, the price of each item, and get a store employee's initials. **(22)** If students chose an item that came in a package, the price of the entire package was to be recorded.

The students could look for items over the weekend. On Monday, they would meet and compare bargains. In the end, the student who had the lowest price total for all the combined items would win two movie tickets. **(23)** The economics class met on Monday. Kamal had the highest total. He listed a pair of hair barrettes for $5.45, a video game for $21.00, a leather belt with a metal buckle for $35.00, and a shirt for $18.99. If Kamal had bought these items, he would have spent a total of $80.44, plus tax!

(24) Kim thought that she would be the winner. Her total was less than $10.00. She had found a headband for $1.19, a slide whistle for $2.49, a metal toy car for $2.08, and a washcloth for $1.88.

Just as Kim was about to claim her prize, Dave announced that he had broken the rules by spending money. He reported that he spent only $1.99, however. Holding up a package of ponytail holders that he had bought for his sister, he explained. **(25)** The bands fastened hair they were made of stretch cotton, and each was held together by a metal clamp. To demonstrate how they were musical, he stretched one as far as he could, strummed it, and sang along.

  CHAPTER TEST

Combining Sentences

COMBINING FOR VARIETY

DIRECTIONS Combine each of the following sets of sentences. In some cases
you will add, delete, or change some words to make smooth combinations.
Use the headings above each set of sentences to guide you. Make your
corrections between the lines.

Example The leading story focused on a dog that could bark "I Did It My

Way." ~~He barked the song~~ while he balanced on his front paws.

Inserting Adjectives, Adverbs, and Prepositional Phrases

1. Micah enjoys playing tennis and volleyball with her friends. Her friends have a lot of energy.

2. Some authors write by drawing on their personal experience. They write truthfully.

3. Simon has been taking clarinet lessons. The clarinet lessons are in the Fine Arts Building.

4. Water conservation is studied by students from rural areas. It is also studied by students from

large cities.

Using Participial and Absolute Phrases

5. The lightning struck. The ancient oak tree crashed to the ground.

6. Warren practiced his violin every day. He wanted to become a concert violinist.

7. The defendant nodded his head. The defendant admitted his guilt.

8. The critic applauded wildly. He was delighted by the new play.

Using Appositive Phrases

9. Abby tried out for the drama team her freshman year at college. She is an accomplished

actress.

10. At nightfall, the caravan rolled into the town. The town was a cluster of old buildings.

11. Dieter is our new foreign exchange student. Dieter comes from Sweden.

12. Have you met Mr. Guerro? He is our new Spanish teacher.

Coordinating Ideas

13. The librarian stamped the book. Then she told the student the due date.

14. Great customer service helps to increase sales. A knowledgeable sales staff also helps to increase sales.

15. The student composed sonatas. He also composed symphonies.

16. Carleen gave me a bouquet of flowers. She also gave a bouquet to Modena.

Subordinating Ideas

17. Some people learn to cook. Some people enjoy eating good food.

18. Paperbacks these days are so inexpensive. Students can build a good library at home.

19. The senator failed to realize the trouble. The trouble was in the local districts, not the state capital.

20. Cathy is the best candidate for class president. Cathy has served well on quite a few committees.

REVISING A PASSAGE

DIRECTIONS The following passage needs to be revised. Make your corrections in the right margin or on a separate sheet of paper. Use what you have learned to combine sentences in the passage in the following ways:

- Inserting prepositional phrases
- Using participial phrases
- Coordinating ideas
- Subordinating ideas

                    Knowing that

Example Joseph wanted to see the new dinosaur exhibit at the museum downtown. Molly invited him to go with her ~~to the exhibit.~~

Grandma's Garden

We lived next door to my grandma. Grandma was the best cook in the world. Who would have thought that green beans could taste so good or that you could make a meal out of corn bread and lima beans? Somehow Grandma managed to make everything taste like a special treat. She had a huge garden out behind her house, and she grew every kind of vegetable she could find.

She began her garden each year. She raked out all the old dead leaves and roots from the previous year. She started preparing the ground for planting. We helped by bringing in a load of compost and fertilizer and mixing it with the topsoil that was already there. Next, she set up the rows. Then she hoed the soil into small mountain ranges that ran the length of the garden.

The next step in planting was to bring in the seed. She opened a packet of seeds. Then she placed the seeds a few inches apart in the row. My cousins and I then blanketed the seeds lightly with a little topsoil. We continued planting and covering until all the rows were planted. Next, she watered each row every day until the young plants began to peek above the ground. Within ten days, the garden looked like a regiment of small green soldiers standing at attention.

Grandma then cultivated each row until the plants began to blossom. Our job, when the vegetables were ripe, was to pick all the green beans. She handed each of us a small basket. When we said we were finished, she walked. She walked along the rows. She inspected our work and called our attention to all the pods we had missed.

We enjoyed those days working side by side with the best gardener and cook in town.

Improving Sentence Style

REVISING FOR VARIETY

DIRECTIONS   The style of the following sentences needs to be improved.
Use what you have learned about varying sentence beginnings, sentence
structure, and wordy sentences to make your revisions. Make your
revisions between the lines. Use the headings above each set of sentences to
guide you.

Example   ~~Joan was~~ excited and nervous ~~as she~~ prepared to leave for her
first experience as a foreign exchange student.

Varying Sentence Beginnings

1. The editors worked around the clock to finish correcting all the essays in one week.

2. Alicia was unstoppable at the tennis tournament.

3. Justin awkwardly looked at the ground and shuffled his feet in the snow.

4. The insurance adjustors examined the scene of the accident carefully and said that both

drivers were at fault.

5. The copy editor altered the wording and produced a new sentence.

Revising Wordy Sentences

6. The capital of Thailand is commonly referred to as Bangkok.

7. As for the doctors in Thailand, there is one doctor for every 4,843 people.

8. The language that the people in Thailand speak and use is called Thai.

9. The government that the people of Thailand have is known as a democracy.

10. When people use money in Thailand, the currency that the people in Thailand always buy

and sell with is called baht.

Revising Sentences Through Reduction

11. At the time the first team was ready to enter the field, the other team decided that they would

forfeit the game.

12. Randy rode in the parade in spite of the fact that he knew that his car had a noisy muffler.

13. Many people seem to enjoy going to air shows due to the fact that they can come and go as they please.

14. In the event that the first service line is busy, please call the alternate number to receive your account information.

15. Due to the fact that we are short on time, I think we should ride into town by means of a taxi.

Varying Sentence Structure

16. Reading improvement is now offered. It is offered in many colleges. Students take this course to improve their reading speed. The classes also improve their reading comprehension.

17. Some mystery books give great clues throughout the course of the story. Other mystery books do not allow the reader to determine who the villain is until the very end.

18. An orchestra has many parts. One section is called the strings. Another section is called the percussion. Still another section is called the brass. The last section is called the woodwinds.

19. Sometimes people from coastal states visit high mountain areas. They have difficulty breathing. They are not accustomed to the thinner air and the higher altitude.

20. The Pulitzer Prize in drama is awarded every year. The award is coveted by many playwrights. These playwrights are professionals.

REVISING A PASSAGE

DIRECTIONS The following passage needs to be revised. Make your corrections between the lines. Use what you have learned to combine sentences in the passage in the following ways:

- Vary sentence beginnings
- Revise wordy sentences
- Revise sentences through reduction
- Vary sentence structure

Example ~~The~~ Independence Square *In the center of town is* ~~is in the center of town. Many~~ *where many* people enjoy all types of entertainment ~~there.~~

Accra, Capital of Ghana

The largest city in Ghana is Accra. It is also the capital city of Ghana, located in the western plateau region of Africa. Accra is a modern city with a population of more than one million. Accra lies on the northern coast of the Gulf of Guinea. It is a short distance from the equator.

Transportation in Accra is similar to that in any major city. An international airport links Accra to business and trade all over the world. If you want to travel from Accra to the interior regions of Africa, you have to travel by means of the extensive railroad system. City transportation consists of automobiles and bicycles. On any given business day, the streets are crowded with people walking to work.

Accra is home to a great variety of gathering places, such as the International Conference Centre, a sports stadium, and Independence Square. The largest meeting place is Independence Square. It is surrounded by the State House, the stadium and local and national government offices. The square can accommodate crowds of over 25,000 people.

Fine arts centers and museums are plentiful in Accra. Music, dancing, art, and theater events are regularly held in the Art Centre and in the National Theatre. The National Museum and the Centre for National Culture regularly exhibit traditional handicrafts, and they have historical artifacts as well.

People who live in Accra can enjoy the special attractions, the beautiful view of the sea, and the annual festivals. Those who visit will be welcomed by the friendly people who live there.

Understanding Paragraphs and Compositions

UNDERSTANDING PARAGRAPHS

DIRECTIONS Use what you have learned about paragraphs to answer the items in the right column on pp. 66–67.

Paragraph 1

One of the largest climatic zones in South America is the tropical rain forest, which covers approximately forty percent of South America. The main contributor to the size of the rain forest is the Amazon River. The Amazon stretches across a little over four thousand miles of the northern portion of South America and traverses three connecting countries: Peru, Brazil, and Colombia. The rain forest, which is a humid seventy to ninety degrees most of the year and has an average rainfall of seventy-nine inches, supports amazingly diverse plant and animal life. However, few people live in the rain forest. Its large size and biological diversity make the rain forest an important climatic zone.

Paragraph 2

The northern grassland area is close to the equator and the tropical rain forests. This large expanse of tropical grassland is perfect for grazing cattle. The grassland, the second largest climatic zone in South America, is found in both the northern and the southern regions of the continent. Temperate grassland supports hardwood forests and fertile land for farms and ranches. The southern grassland is generally temperate; it reaches from Argentina into Paraguay. However, the southern grassland includes the hottest area of South America.

Curtain Up: Movement for the Stage

Have you ever seen an actor barely move his arms when the scene requires that he extend his arm in a sweeping gesture? He looks more like a penguin flapping his flippers tightly at his side than like a man making an important point. Unfortunately, such an actor may never have studied movement for the theatrical stage. Acting students are required to take courses in exercise and movement to help them develop a full range of motions they can use to prepare for a role. Instructors teach a variety of physical movements along with different theatrical movement styles. They encourage students to connect voice and physical movement and to look at the relationship between a character's spoken lines and physical movements. Movement impacts the meaning of each line. In addition,

---

PARAGRAPH 1

1. What is the main idea of the paragraph?

____

____

____

2. Cross out the sentence that is not related to the main idea.

3. What types of supporting details are used—sensory details, facts, statistics, examples, anecdotes?

____

PARAGRAPH 2

4. Number the sentences in this paragraph so they appear in the best order.

5. Which type of order is used—chronological, logical, or order of importance?

____

CURTAIN UP

6. Check the technique used in the introduction.
___ anecdote
___ startling fact
___ idea or opinion
___ a question
___ vivid description
___ quotation

most theater classes cover changes in movement through different historical periods. Studying the variations allows students to see how movement has evolved and lets them expand their movement repertoires. They also learn to understand the different ways actors have been treated by society over the last few centuries.

Most acting students leave their movement classes feeling that they have a much better understanding of the work involved in creating a fully developed character.

Revised introduction: ____

____

ANALYZING THESIS STATEMENTS

DIRECTIONS Each one of the following sentences presents a topic, but not a main idea about the topic. Rewrite each thesis statement to make it more effective.

Example Computers have broadened the scope of communication.

Although computers have broadened the scope of communication, some people prefer face-to-face interaction.

1. Safety is important in a research laboratory.

____

____

2. Different personalities affect each work environment.

____

____

3. There are many ways to choose a college.

____

____

4. Television commercials present a variety of products.

____

____

5. Some people are falsely accused of crimes.

____

____

7. Rewrite the introduction on the lines provided, using a different technique.

____

____

8. Identify one direct reference and one transitional expression.

____

____

9. Use the paragraph symbol (¶) to indicate where a new paragraph should begin.

10. Cross out the sentence that interferes with the unity of the piece.

11. What kind of order is used—chronological, spatial, order of importance, logical?

____

12. What technique is used in the conclusion—restatement of thesis, call to action, reference to introduction, summary, example? Explain your answer.

____

____

____

WRITING AN INFORMATIVE COMPOSITION

DIRECTIONS   Use the facts presented in note form below to help you
write a brief composition on a separate sheet of paper. You may not need to
use all the information, and you may want to add additional information
through personal knowledge. Be sure to keep your paper to the limited topic
and to elaborate your main idea sufficiently. Include a thesis statement
for the composition, topic sentences for each supporting paragraph, and a
concluding paragraph.

The Organic Approach to a Healthier Yard

1. Organic approach: will cut back on the labor of lawn maintenance; does not use poison; the

   grass will be strong enough to protect itself from major weed problems

2. Sharpen mower blades: dull blades tear grass, easier for grass to catch diseases when it is torn;

   gives the grass a dull look; sharpening blades is not expensive

3. Cut to a height of 2.5 to 3 inches: short grass is weak grass; taller grass looks thicker; plants

   need surface area to take in light; leave grass clippings on the grass—they fertilize it

4. Don't water too much; one good soaking a week or rain; too much water makes shallow roots

5. Punch holes in the yard (aerate); packed soil does not get good water, nutrients, or root growth

6. Corn-gluten meal kills weed seeds; do not use on a new yard—also kills new grass seed

7. Some weeds have deep roots; need to dig out at least four to five inches of the root; keep grass

   2 1/2 inches high; height of grass will also shade many weeds and keep them from growing

8. Cover the bald spots; sow grass seeds on bare spots; inhibits new weed growth

9. Spread about one pound of nitrogen compost for every 1,000 square feet; too much nitrogen

   will allow grass to grow too fast and roots will not reach down far enough into the ground

10. Don't fertilize too often; fertilize in spring and early fall; grass clippings count for about half of

    the fertilization needed

Reading Workshop: Reflective Essay

DIRECTIONS Read the following passage, and answer the questions in the right-hand column.

Louder Than Words

The day after I arrived home from my first semester of college, I awoke to a soft clank beside me. Turning my sleepy gaze toward the sound, I noticed a coffee cup sitting on my night stand. My father, in his tattered flannel bathrobe and scuffed slippers, had set it there. "Morning," he said. "Breakfast is cooking." He stood there long enough to make eye contact, just to make sure I was awake. Then he shuffled down the creaky stairs to pour a cup of coffee for himself. For a moment I was irritated. How could my father say so little to me? After all, he had not seen me in four months. Then I rolled over on my side and lifted the steaming mug to my lips. I appreciated the light, creamy color—just enough milk. Then I tasted it: no sugar, just the way I like it. In that moment I knew that despite his silence, Dad was glad to have me there. As usual, his actions spoke louder than his words.

Dad has never been good at discussing his feelings. He grew up around men who showed their affection by bringing home the monthly paycheck and supporting the athletic interests of their children. Dad has always worked long hours, yet he made sure to attend every single game when I pitched for my high school team. I could always find him leaning forward with his intent, penetrating gaze. He did not jump up and down like other parents. If we won, he said, "Good job, Son." If we lost, he said we would do better next time. Other than that, we never talked about my game.

During that visit home, I realized how Dad really felt about my baseball career—and about me—when I dug into the bottom drawer of his desk. Instead of the writing paper I was looking for, I found

1. Which words and phrases in the first paragraph express the writer's emotions?

____

____

____

____

2. In the second paragraph, what do you learn about the writer's father from the father's actions?

____

____

____

____

3. In the second paragraph, what is the purpose of including the father's words?

____

____

____

____

an overstuffed folder, brimming with newspaper clippings and photos. The photos were of me pitching my first no-hitter, smiling triumphantly when we won the championship, and riding high on the shoulders of my teammates. My eyes began to sting as I leafed through the yellowed pictures. They told me what he has never managed to say: He loves me and is really proud of me.

Now when I think about Dad, I realize how his ways have influenced me. Unlike Dad, I tell people what they mean to me, but like him, I try to show my feelings through my actions, so people will know that my words really mean something. Sometimes I make my girlfriend's old car shine like a new penny or help my mom prune wilted leaves from her begonias. And I do something special for Dad. These days when I am home for a visit, I try to get up before he does. When he comes downstairs, the coffee is freshly prepared, and there is a cup at his place at the table: black, with sugar—just the way he likes it.

4. What does the writer learn about his father?

____

____

____

____

____

5. Who in your life reminds you of the narrator's father? Why?

____

____

____

____

____

DIRECTIONS Use examples and ideas from the passage you have just read to complete the graphic organizer.

Analyzing Expressive Style

▶ ELEMENTS	▶ EXAMPLE	▶ HOW THE EXAMPLE CLARIFIES THE NARRATOR'S THOUGHTS AND FEELINGS
First-person point of view		
Words that express feelings		
Words and phrases that echo common speech		
Evocative language (words with strong connotations, sensory details, figures of speech that evoke emotion)	*"Sometimes I make my girlfriend's old car shine like a new penny. . . ."*	*This simile helps readers see how hard the narrator works on his girlfriend's car. We can tell from that how much he cares about his girlfriend.*

Writing Workshop: Reflective Essay

DIRECTIONS Use the following guidelines to help you revise and correct the essay on the next page.

THE INTRODUCTION SHOULD

- grab the reader's attention

- supply necessary background information, including an introduction of the subject

- hint at the subject's significance

THE BODY SHOULD

- include anecdotes that illustrate the subject's significance

- effectively order events and details

THE CONCLUSION SHOULD

- reveal the significance of the subject

REMEMBER TO

- ❑ use colloquialisms to reflect the way people actually speak, to establish setting, or to characterize people

- ❑ punctuate dialogue correctly

Writing Workshop: Revising and Proofreading

DIRECTIONS The following essay has been written in response to this prompt:

Write an essay about a person who has had a significant effect on your life.

The reflective essay contains problems in style, organization, and punctuation.

- Use the space between the lines to revise the essay and correct the errors.
- If you cannot fit some of your revisions between the lines, rewrite the revised sections on a separate piece of paper.

Mrs. McCarthy's Magic

When I first walked into Mrs. McCarthy's third-grade class, my knees rattled. It was my first day in public school, and I was nervous. Mrs. McCarthy turned out to be a special teacher.

> **a.** Problem with statement of subject's significance

Mrs. McCarthy participated in service projects all over town and always shared stories about her experiences. One day she told us that there were people downtown who did not have enough to eat. "I know that it is a true thing," she said, "because every weekend I work at a soup kitchen downtown." My classmates and I sat on the edges of our seats. As she described the soup kitchen, I imagined her behind a counter, smiling at the people who came by.

> **b.** Problem with colloquialisms

The morning after I filled my shoe box, I felt warm inside as I placed it on Mrs. McCarthy's desk. I had learned the joy of giving, because Mrs. McCarthy knew how to teach me to give.

> **c.** Problem with paragraph order

Would you like to help these people, too? Mrs. McCarthy asked.

She bustled over to the closet at the back of the room and pulled out

shoe boxes and art supplies. We decorated the boxes, and she asked

us to think about small things that a hungry person might need.

After school I took my box home and filled it with packets of soup

and cocoa, cans of tuna, a plastic mug, a spoon, toothbrushes, and

toothpaste.

> **d.** Problem with punctuation

Mrs. McCarthy does not teach third grade anymore. But I think

of her whenever I use the lessons she taught me. For my senior serv-

ice project, I volunteer twice a week as a reading tutor. While I help

students practice reading, I also try to be a positive influence in

whatever way I can. Yesterday a young girl named Sarah was wor-

ried because her mother seemed stressed and tired lately from

working two jobs. I gently assured her that there were some small

ways she could help. Together we made a card for her mother to let

her know her hard work was appreciated. When I help children

with a project like this, I know I'm teaching a skill that is just as

important as writing and math; I'm teaching them ways to show

they care for the people around them.

for **CHAPTER 22** `page 632`   **TEST**

Reading Workshop: Short Story

DIRECTIONS Read the following passage, and answer the questions in the right-hand column.

Good Morning

When I was a boy, I walked through two miles of woods to get to our schoolhouse, and I would take my father's twenty-two rifle with me and hide it in a hollow tree before I got to the schoolhouse, and get it as I came home in the evening.

One evening, coming from school, I ran into a community uprising at Mr. Epperly's house. Mr. Epperly's cow had gone mad and was bawling lonesome bawls and twisting the young apple trees out of the ground with her horns, and the whole community was demanding that Mr. Epperly's dog, Old Ranger, be shot as Old Ranger had fought and killed the mad dog that bit the cow.

Mr. Epperly wanted to know if it wouldn't be safe to put Old Ranger in the stable or someplace and keep him penned up until the danger period was over, but the neighbors said no; that Mr. Epperly's children might slip and feed him through the cracks and get bit.

Mr. Epperly said he could not do it himself, and wanted to know who would volunteer to do it, but none of the men would.

Mr. Epperly came to me, and said, "Joe, why can't you take him with you through the woods on your way home and do it?"

I told Mr. Epperly I did not want to shoot Old Ranger. I saw Mr. Epperly's three kids were already keeping close to the old dog.

Mr. Epperly then pulled a one-dollar bill from his pocket.

"I will give you this dollar bill if you'll do it," he said.

I considered. I had never yet had a one-dollar bill all my own and while the idea of shooting Old Ranger did not appeal to me, it did seem like a thing that was demanded by the whole community, and they all put at me to do it, trying to make me feel like a kind

1. What adjectives would you use to describe Joe, the narrator?

____

____

____

____

of hero, and pointed to the danger to Mr. Epperly's children. Then

Mr. Epperly put a piece of clothesline around Old Ranger's neck

and I started with him. The Epperly kids began to cry.

As I walked through the woods by the little path, I started look-

ing for a place suitable to shoot a dog and leave him lay. I saw a

heavy clump of wild grapevines, and I led him down under there

and then got back up in the path. Old Ranger looked at me and

whined and wagged his tail. He wanted to come to me. I recollected

always seeing him wherever there was a splash of sunshine in

Mr. Epperly's yard when I would pass there and Mr. Epperly's kids

would join me for school.

I went down and untied Old Ranger and walked on. I came to a

place where there was a hickory grove in a little flat where the

underbrush was thin. I recollected how Old Ranger liked to go to

the hickory groves and tree squirrels. I led Old Ranger down and

tied him close to the trunk of a big hickory tree.

I started to take aim, but Old Ranger started prancing and

looking up the tree. I remembered then hearing Mr. Epperly tell

how Old Ranger would do that when he'd tree a squirrel and

Mr. Epperly would raise the gun to shoot, and I could not fool Old

Ranger like that.

Besides, there was too much light and Old Ranger could see me

take aim. I decided to wait for the gloom. Soon as the sun dropped a

few more feet behind the Wilson Ridge, there would be gloom, and

maybe Old Ranger would not see so plainly how I pointed the gun.

While I waited for the gloom, the burning started in my pocket. I

took the one-dollar bill out. I had a feeling there was something

nasty about it.

While I thought of that, Old Ranger reared and barked and

surged at the cord leash, and when I looked back out the path I saw

2. How does Joe feel about Old Ranger? How can you tell?

____

____

____

____

____

Mr. Epperly's three kids, but they were running away. They had turned to run when Old Ranger barked. I guessed they had slipped off from their house and followed just to see where I left Old Ranger.

The thought struck me that they would run back to their house and tell I had not shot Old Ranger yet, and that would set the folks to worrying again, and I took aim. I thought I had better fire in their hearing. I took aim at Old Ranger, but I could not touch the trigger the way he looked at me and tried to speak, so I fired in the air so the Epperly kids could say they heard the shot.

I stuck the dollar back in my pocket, went down and hugged Old Ranger around the neck. I knew I would never shoot Old Ranger. I took him and walked on. I got to the edge of our field. I climbed on the gate and sat a long time and considered. I tried to think up how I could explain to my mother why I had brought Old Ranger home with me so that she would not be scared. I could not decide how I could ever explain with a good face that I had a one-dollar bill in my pocket I had been given to shoot Old Ranger.

I remembered where I had seen an empty castor-oil bottle at the edge of the path. It was still there, and I got it, and stuck the one-dollar bill in it, and buried the bottle in some soft dirt under the corner of the fence.

My mother decided that since I had fired the shot, she would let me keep Old Ranger for a month, with the community thinking he was dead, but it was the hardest month I ever spent.

The Epperly kids would not walk with me to school. They would pucker up to cry when they saw me, and the other kids down at the schoolhouse, they would say with a sneer, "What did you buy with your dollar bill?"

3. What characterization technique is used in the paragraph beginning "The thought struck …"?

____

____

____

____

____

4. Why do you think Joe buries the dollar bill?

____

____

____

____

____

5. Why won't the Epperly kids walk to school with Joe?

____

____

____

____

____

I could not answer. I could not tell them about the castor-oil bottle under the fence corner or Old Ranger in our stable; the Epperly kids searched the woods on both sides of the path to our house, hunting for the body of Old Ranger, but they would not ask me where I had left him, and other neighbors spoke of how Old Ranger's great booming voice was missed.

Mrs. Epperly was kind to me. I met her in the road one day, and she told me how she had scolded the kids for treating me like that, "But," she added, "if it was to do over, I would not allow it done. The children . . . Mr. Epperly, too, they're half crazy."

Then came the happy morning. "You can take Old Ranger home now, Joe," my mother said. "Been over a month. No danger now."

I went to the stable, got Old Ranger, and he reared and licked my face. I shouldered my book strap, and led Old Ranger down the path. I stopped at the fence corner and got the castor-oil bottle with the one-dollar bill in it. I had a time trying to hold Old Ranger's mouth shut so I could get in sight of the Epperly house before he barked.

At the right place where they could see us when they came running to the front porch, I let Old Ranger have his voice. Old Ranger let go with a great howl that rolled and rocked across the ridges, and the Epperlys came bounding. Mr. and Mrs. Epperly and the three kids. They alternated between my neck and Old Ranger's, and I don't know to this day which of us got the most hugging.

I handed Mr. Epperly the castor-oil bottle.

"Why did you do that?" he said.

"It felt nasty in my pocket," I said.

He tried to make me keep it and when I wouldn't, he just pitched it toward me and his three kids, and we started for the schoolhouse, feeling rich, with a whole dollar to spend.

—Mark Hager

6. What can you infer about Joe from the events in the story?

____

____

____

____

____

DIRECTIONS Use the ideas and information in the passage you just read to complete the graphic organizer.

Analyzing Characterization

▶ CHARACTERIZATION TECHNIQUES	▶ EXAMPLES
Indirect: The writer describes how the character looks, moves, or dresses.	*"I shouldered my book strap, . . . "*
Indirect: The writer reveals the character's thoughts and feelings.	
Indirect: The writer shows the character's effect on other characters.	
Indirect: The writer shows the character's actions.	

Writing Workshop: Short Story

DIRECTIONS Use the following guidelines to help you revise and correct the short story on the next page.

THE BEGINNING SHOULD

- engage readers

- introduce characters, including a fully fleshed out main character, and establish setting

- set plot in motion with event or situation that initiates conflict

THE MIDDLE SHOULD

- provide setting details that help develop characterization, plot, mood, or symbolism

- tell the story from a consistent point of view

- use sensory details and figures of speech to enhance the vividness and style of the writing

- present events in logical order until the conflict reaches a climax

THE END SHOULD

- move toward resolution

- resolve the conflict, including final details

REMEMBER TO

- ❏ avoid weak modifiers

- ❏ use correct verb tense

for **CHAPTER 22**　`page 641`　　　　　　　　　　　　　　　　　　　　**TEST**

Writing Workshop: Revising and Proofreading

DIRECTIONS The following beginning of a short story was written in response to this prompt:

Write a short story that concerns school.

The story excerpt contains problems in style, organization, and usage.

- Use the space between the lines for revisions and corrections.
- If you cannot fit some of your revisions between the lines, rewrite the revised sections on a separate piece of paper.

The Color of Her Eyes

Character building—that's how her parents described each move they made. Moving was sort of exciting, she thought, but it was lonely. She had to adjust to a new town and a new house and make new friends all over again. This time she couldn't seem to manage the self-reliance and confidence that a new move took.

On the ride to school, the air was cool and the sun was warm; the late autumn weather was pleasantly familiar. Here, the leaves turned the maroon of scrub oak rather than the gold of cottonwood. In the distance, the school loomed gray and foreboding in stark contrast to the pleasant autumn day.

> **a.** Problem with order of paragraphs

Exhausted from unpacking, she had not even dressed for school yet. She grabbed her favorite light-blue sweater and pulled it over her head.

Sighing, she remembered how bright and new her last school building looked. She averted her eyes and spoke to no one after she entered the building. The other students didn't notice her, except

> **b.** Problem with verb tense

one guy who made a crack about her old sweater. A girl sitting next to her in algebra class asked whether her boots were boy's boots.

I attempted to sound casual and tough, "Yeah, work boots, steel-tipped."

Lunch was the worst part of the day. She avoided the loud masses in the noisy cafeteria. Instead, she went to the library and read a book while eating the sandwich she had brought. A library monitor sent her into the dark halls, saying, "You can't eat in here."

Throughout the day, she navigated her way around this imposing new world. Finally, she filed out of her last class with a large stack of books given to her by her teacher "to get on track" with the other students.

She neared her locker and slightly stumbled, dropping all of her books. Disheartened, she bent down to pick them up. As she gathered the books together, a voice nearby said, "Can I help you?" She looked up and stared at a boy with sandy hair. He bent down to help and then said, "Hey, you know your sweater matches the color of your eyes exactly."

c. Problem with point of view

d. Problem with weak modifier

e. Problem with details

for **CHAPTER 23** *page 670*   **TEST**

Reading Workshop: Comparison-Contrast Article

DIRECTIONS Read the following passage, and answer the questions in the right-hand column.

News Coverage of the Great Fairview Flood

If you want to get the latest news, do you turn on the television or open the newspaper? Depending on which medium you choose, you may get a different story. Last fall, the Fairview River flooded its banks, killing seven people and causing millions of dollars in property damage. This event was covered extensively by both television and newspapers. Although television coverage offered startling images of the flood, newspapers were able, with their in-depth coverage, to provide a more thorough examination of the flood's causes and its aftermath.

Attention-getting techniques, like live video, appeared initially to give television an advantage over print media in covering the natural disaster. Television footage showed torrents of water carrying away cars and uprooted trees. This dramatic video, coupled with a voice-over explaining the destruction caused by the flood-waters, painted a powerful image of the disaster. However, the still photography utilized by newspapers also created effective images. One photograph of a survivor clinging to a tree as a rescue helicopter maneuvered above him was as effective in its own way as video coverage.

Both television and newspapers gave the story prominent coverage with a similar slant. Television news broadcasts ran the story first during the worst days of the flooding. Newspapers featured the story on the front page with additional coverage inside the first section. Both concentrated on the causes of the flood and included descriptions of the effects of the damaging waters.

1. What is the stated main idea of this essay?

____

____

____

____

2. What relevant feature is compared in the second paragraph?

____

____

____

____

____

3. What details support the main idea of the third paragraph?

____

____

____

____

Chapter Tests   **75**

In depth of coverage, however, television and newspapers differed markedly. Because network television news broadcasts are limited to a half-hour including commercials, a lead story, like this flood, generally receives only three minutes of coverage. Although some networks ran special reports on the flood, time constraints allowed for only brief interviews with survivors and flood engineers. In addition, television, because it is a primarily visual medium, rarely stays with any interviewee for more than a minute. This also limited television's depth of coverage. Newspapers, on the other hand, ran the story on several pages and included lengthy explanations of the causes of the flood, detailed maps of the flood's path, and extensive interviews with various officials and survivors.

The constraints of time and the medium of television news combined to make its coverage of the Fairview flood more superficial than its print competitor. Reading a detailed lead story from a newspaper provides a clearer picture of this great flood than watching the streaming footage of a newscast.

4. How does the depth of television coverage differ from the depth of newspaper coverage?

____

____

____

____

____

5. What structure does this comparison-contrast essay follow?

____

____

____

____

for **CHAPTER 23** `page 670` *continued* **TEST**

DIRECTIONS Use the information from the passage you have just read to complete the graphic organizer.

Finding Main Ideas

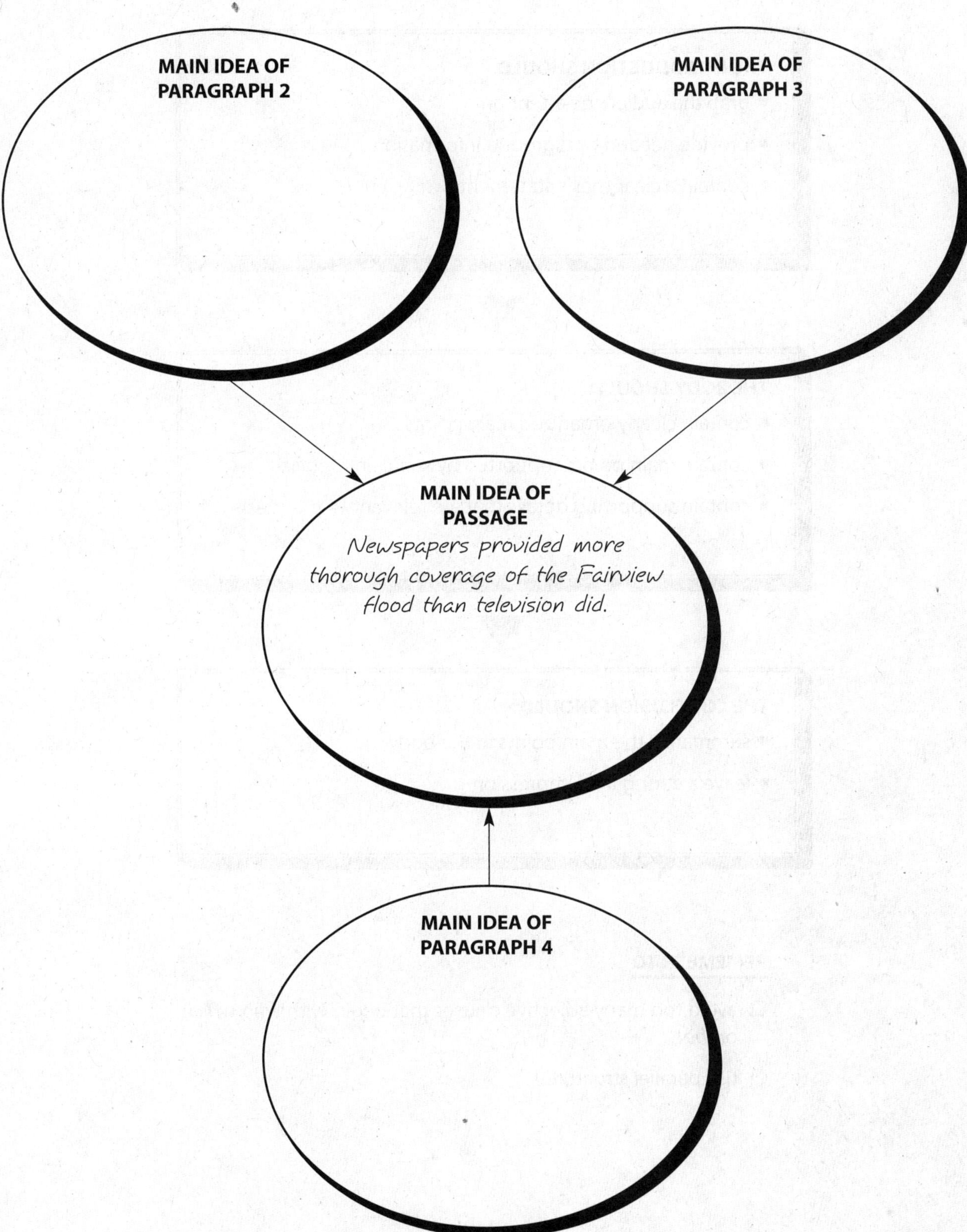

Writing Workshop: Comparison-Contrast Essay

DIRECTIONS Use the following guidelines to help you revise and correct the essay on the next page.

THE INTRODUCTION SHOULD

- grab the audience's attention

- provide needed background information

- contain a clear thesis statement

THE BODY SHOULD

- contain clearly organized main points

- contain main points supported by sufficient details

- contain supporting details that are relevant to the thesis

THE CONCLUSION SHOULD

- summarize the main points in the body

- leave a strong final impression

REMEMBER TO

- ❏ avoid too many adjective clauses that begin with *who, which,* or *that*

- ❏ use parallel structure

Writing Workshop: Revising and Proofreading

DIRECTIONS The following comparison-contrast essay was written in reponse to this prompt:

> **Compare the coverage of a historical event in two different media.**

The essay contains problems in style, content, and grammar.

- Use the space between the lines to revise the essay and correct the errors.
- If you cannot fit some of your revisions between the lines, rewrite the revised sections on a separate piece of paper.

Print and Internet: Two Views of Mount Everest

Why didn't the world celebrate the day Edmund Hillary and Tenzing Norgay became the first known humans to reach the summit of the world's highest mountain? Although Hillary and Norgay reached the summit of Everest on May 29, 1953, four days passed before news of their achievement broke in the *Times* of London. By the spring of 2003, media coverage of Everest expeditions was much different. The Internet allowed the public at large to follow—almost hour by hour—the expedition that included the youngest climber ever to reach the peak of Everest, 21-year-old Jess Roskelly.

a. Problem with thesis statement

Watching the frequent Internet updates was more intense than to read the weekly reports in the print media. Online sources provided journal-style coverage of the expedition. Bulletins were filed on a daily basis and up-to-the-minute photos and video of the day's events were available for viewers. Because of the speed of Internet connections, readers who wanted the latest news could learn about

b. Problem with parallel structure

events unfolding on the mountain hours and even days before print sources could report the story. Internet users who wanted to gain greater insight into events could chat online with actual climbers.

Newspapers and newsmagazines reported facts, showed photos of the climbers, and interviewed loved ones, but their stories were old news to Internet users. Internet users could read about the thousands of adventurers who have climbed Everest since Hillary and Norgay's successful ascent. The print media could spend more time gathering facts and editing their content, but their stories were not as timely as those on the Internet. Despite in-depth interviews with loved ones and friends, their stories could not capture the immediacy of online chats and real-time reporting.

c. Problem with supporting details

For days and weeks following the climb, print reporters continued to gather facts and putting their stories together. With a click of a mouse, however, thousands—maybe millions—had already stepped out of their homes into the exhilarating, deadly air above Everest's Camp Four.

d. Problem with parallel structure

Reading Workshop: Causal Analysis

DIRECTIONS Read the following passage, and answer the questions in the right-hand column.

The Effects of High-Protein, Low-Carbohydrate Diets: A Lose-Lose Proposition?

As new research is done, nutritional information grows and changes, but diet plans for weight loss tend to be recycled regardless of their effectiveness. For over three decades, researchers, nutritionists, diet-book authors, and dieters have debated the merits and dangers of a high-protein, low-carbohydrate diet.

There is ample anecdotal evidence of drastic weight loss by dieters who give up pasta, bread, rice, and many vegetables in favor of steak, butter, ham, and eggs: A Kansas man lost 50 pounds in a year, Internet chat room participants claim it is the only plan that works, and neighbors and friends tout the quick-loss benefits of the plan. Yet none of the anecdotes provide clear, scientific answers regarding the diet's long-term effects and potential health risks.

Advocates and detractors agree that weight loss on a high-protein, low-carbohydrate diet can be quick and dramatic, but detractors argue that this loss is often short-lived. Because stored carbohydrates contain large amounts of water, initial weight loss associated with high-protein diets is mostly water rather than fat. In addition, these trendy diets often recommend severely limited food choices and a very low-calorie regimen. Some high-protein diets suggest consuming only 800–1,200 calories per day, even though the Center for Cardiovascular Education puts caloric need for an overweight, dieting individual at ten times that person's current weight. A 160-pound person, for example, needs 1,600 calories a day to lose weight reasonably. Consequently, to maintain the drastic, initial weight loss achieved with the high-protein, low-carbohydrate diet, a

1. What does the title lead you to expect in the rest of the essay?

____

____

____

____

____

2. What causes the drastic, initial weight loss in a high-protein, low-carbohydrate diet?

____

____

____

____

____

3. In the third paragraph, what is one implied cause of why the weight loss is short-lived?

____

____

____

____

____

person would have to deprive his or her body of the nutrients and energy it needs.

A high-protein, low-carbohydrate diet can affect one's long-term health in many negative ways. Underconsumption of calories and carbohydrates leads to ketosis, an abnormal metabolic state in which the body—reacting as though it were starving—begins burning its lean muscle and organ tissue for fuel. Ketosis also puts stress on the kidneys, forcing them to work overtime to maintain a normal blood pH. This condition is called acidosis, and it destroys the kidneys' filtering ability, resulting in excretion of large amounts of bone material and calcium through the urine. The prolonged loss of calcium leads to osteoporosis, a loss of bone tissue, and prolonged kidney stress eventually leads to kidney failure.

A high-protein, low-carbohydrate diet "tricks" the body into weight loss and has the potential for long-term harm. For ongoing health and fitness, one dietary plan is effective and safe: regular exercise and a sensible, well-balanced diet.

4. What causative verbs can be found in the fourth paragraph?

____

____

____

____

5. Why might the author claim that high-protein diets "trick" the body into weight loss?

____

____

____

____

____

DIRECTIONS Use the effects in the fourth paragraph of the passage you have just read to complete the graphic organizer.

Analyzing Cause-and-Effect Structures

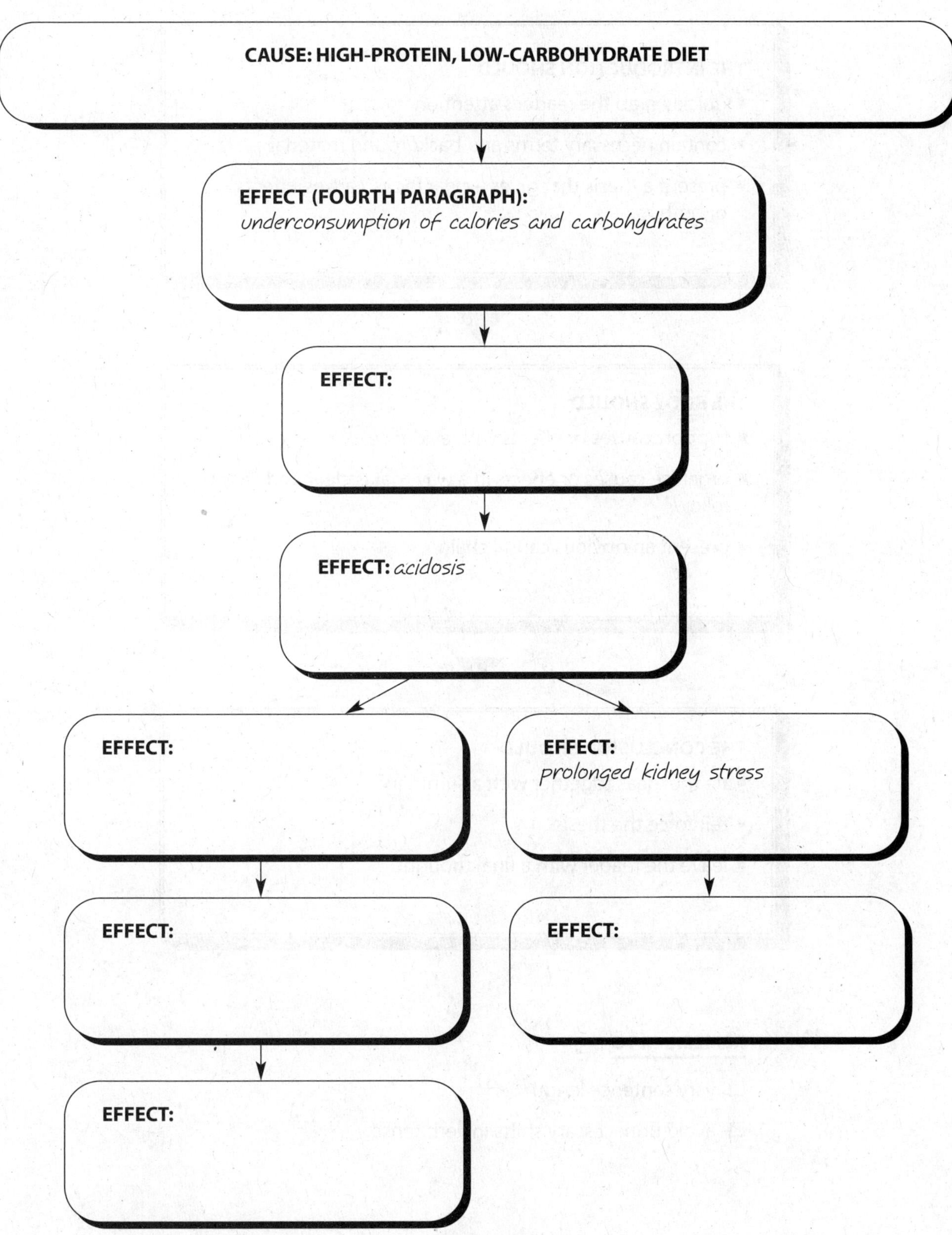

Writing Workshop: Causal Analysis

DIRECTIONS Use the following guidelines to help you revise and correct the analysis on the next page.

THE INTRODUCTION SHOULD

- quickly grab the reader's attention

- contain necessary terms and background material

- present a thesis that gives a clear focus: causes, effects, or both

THE BODY SHOULD

- support causes or effects with evidence

- organize causes or effects in a way that is clear and easy to follow

- present an obvious causal chain

THE CONCLUSION SHOULD

- tie the ideas together with a summary

- reinforce the thesis

- leave the reader with a final thought

REMEMBER TO

- ❑ vary sentence length

- ❑ avoid unnecessary shifts in verb tense

Writing Workshop: Revising and Proofreading

DIRECTIONS The following causal analysis was written in response to this prompt:

> **Write a causal analysis concerning the topic of animals.**

This analysis contains problems in style, content, and grammar.

- Use the space between the lines to revise the analysis and correct the errors.
- If you cannot fit some of your revisions between the lines, rewrite the revised sections on a separate piece of paper.

Where Have All the Frogs Gone?

In many places across the globe, scientists have noticed a troubling trend. Entire species of frogs are disappearing, and much higher-than-normal percentages are developing mutations. So what is causing frogs across the globe to die out and develop deformities? No study pinpoints any single cause, but to date, the identified causes included fungus, parasites, UV-B radiation, and water contamination.

a. Problem with verb tense

Researcher Karen Lips identified fungus as the cause of a large die-off of frogs in a forest reserve in Panama. The fungus covered the skin of the frogs. Frogs breathe through their skin. The fungus blocked their air supply.

b. Problem with sentence style

Studies at Claremont McKenna College found that the flatworm parasite invades at the tadpole stage and interferes with the development of frogs' hind legs. The parasite's primary host is an aquatic snail, so an increase in the abundance of that snail matched an increase in the parasite-related deformities.

c. Problem with missing topic sentence

Another cause of dying species is increased radiation from the sun. Andrew Blaustein showed in laboratory tests that frogs' eggs protected from ultraviolet rays were more likely to hatch than unprotected eggs. The theory is that due to a decrease in the amount of ozone in the upper atmosphere, more UV-B radiation is able to reach the earth's surface. The higher level of radiation from the sun's rays kills off frog eggs that lie on the surface of the water.

From studying sites in Minnesota, the National Institutes of Health (NIH) found that contaminated water is another cause of deformities in frogs. When the frog embryos are exposed to dilutions of water from the affected sites, more than 50 percent develop severe deformities. The NIH is still working to determine whether chemicals or a natural product such as algae is the contaminant.

As scientists continue to research the causes of frog die-offs and mutations, they hope to find answers that might protect other species from potential harm.

d. Problem with conclusion

Reading Workshop: Literary Analysis of a Drama

DIRECTIONS Read the following passage, and answer the questions in the right-hand column.

The Discontent of Jimmy Porter

During the Angry Young Men literary movement of the 1950s and 1960s, British writers expressed disdain for the rigid class structure of their country and for the hypocrisy of upper- and middle-class values. Jimmy Porter, the protagonist of John Osborne's play *Look Back in Anger*, became the poster boy for the Angry Young Men movement. Although Jimmy's savage, bitter words seem to imply action, he never actually does anything, and, therefore, never really becomes the hero the audience wants him to be.

In his early twenties, Jimmy has working-class roots and a university education. He is married to Alison, a woman who comes from the middle class. Although his education entitles him to the middle-class status that his wife is accustomed to, he is still emotionally attached to his origins. Consequently, he has chosen a living that does not require a university education—running a candy stand. Osborne intended for Jimmy's personality to reflect the ambiguity of his social status, and, in the stage directions, he describes Jimmy as a "disconcerting mixture of sincerity and cheerful malice, of tenderness and freebooting cruelty; restless, importunate, full of pride, a combination which alienates the sensitive and insensitive alike" (Osborne 9–10).

When Jimmy sits down with the Sunday newspaper—the high point of his week—he reads articles that contribute to the primary causes of his anger: the British class structure and his inability to change his situation. Jimmy represents many working-class people who obtained high levels of education, but found that class barriers were still raised against them (Hinchliffe 9). Placed in such a

1. Why does Jimmy run a candy stand, in the writer's view?

____

____

____

____

____

2. According to the writer, why is Jimmy angry?

____

____

____

____

____

scenario, Jimmy has no sense of identity and feels alienated from both classes. His anger is heightened by a consciousness of its futility. He tells his wife and a friend, "I learnt at an early age what it was to be angry—angry and helpless. And I can never forget it" (Osborne 58).

Jimmy believes that the only place he can exert some control is in his personal relationships, and as a result, he is very cruel to Alison. He belittles her with statements like "She hasn't had a thought for years" (Osborne 12), and he describes her as "clumsy" to his friend Cliff (24). Viewing Alison's mother as the embodiment of middle-class hypocrisy, he shouts at Alison that her mother "ought to be dead" (53). Yet Jimmy can't sustain his anger, even on this level. Frequently, after he lashes out at Alison, the couple play a childish game of make-believe, pretending to be a squirrel and a bear. Their game is "[a] silly symphony for people who couldn't bear the pain of being human beings any longer" (47).

At the conclusion of the play, it is unlikely that Jimmy's problems will be solved. He is as helpless and disappointed in the last scene of the play as he was in the first. Although the dialogue reveals Jimmy's suffering and his anger at his predicament, Jimmy never changes anything in his life. In the end, Jimmy and Alison withdraw into their own make-believe world, and the unresolved anger remains to haunt the reader.

Works Cited

Hinchliffe, Arnold. *John Osborne*. New York: Twayne, 1984.

Osborne, John. *Look Back in Anger*. New York: Penguin, 1957.

3. Is the source of the quotation in the third paragraph a primary source or a secondary source?

____

____

____

____

4. What idea do the descriptive details quoted at the beginning of the fourth paragraph support?

____

____

____

____

____

5. What main point does the last quotation in the fourth paragraph support?

____

____

____

____

____

Elements of Language | Sixth Course

DIRECTIONS Use the ideas and information in the passage you have just read to complete the graphic organizer.

Paraphrasing

▶ **ORIGINAL**	▶ **PARAPHRASE**
In his early twenties, Jimmy has working-class roots and a university education. He is married to Alison, a woman who comes from the middle class. Although his education entitles him to the middle-class status that his wife is accustomed to, he is still emotionally attached to his origins. Consequently, he has chosen a living that does not require a university education—running a candy stand. Osborne intended for Jimmy's personality to reflect the ambiguity of his social status, and, in the stage directions, he describes Jimmy as a "disconcerting mixture of sincerity and cheerful malice, of tenderness and freebooting cruelty; restless, importunate, full of pride, a combination which alienates the sensitive and insensitive alike" (Osborne 9–10).	*Jimmy comes from a working-class background but has been educated in a university. He is married to a middle-class woman named Alison, and his marriage to her would give him access to the middle class. Because he is attached to his working-class roots, however, he runs a candy stand. This type of job does not require a university education. In the stage directions, the description of Jimmy reveals the discord that he feels about his class struggle. He is described there as having a strange mixture of characteristics like pride and hostility and cruelty and tenderness.*
Jimmy believes that the only place he can exert some control is in his personal relationships, and as a result, he is very cruel to Alison. He belittles her with statements like "She hasn't had a thought for years" (Osborne 12), and he describes her as "clumsy" to his friend Cliff (24). Viewing Alison's mother as the embodiment of middle-class hypocrisy, he shouts at Alison that her mother "ought to be dead" (53). Yet Jimmy can't sustain his anger, even on this level. Frequently, after he lashes out at Alison, the couple play a childish game of make-believe, pretending to be a squirrel and a bear. Their game is "[a] silly symphony for people who couldn't bear the pain of being human beings any longer" (47).	

Writing Workshop: Literary Analysis of a Drama

DIRECTIONS Use the following guidelines to help you revise and correct the literary analysis on the next page.

THE INTRODUCTION SHOULD

- contain the author's name, the title of the play, and necessary background information

- include a thesis statement

THE BODY SHOULD

- include at least two major points to support the thesis, with evidence from the play to prove the points

- appropriately organize the major points and supporting evidence

THE CONCLUSION SHOULD

- summarize the thesis and bring the essay to a satisfying close

---

REMEMBER TO

- ❑ correctly integrate, or work, short quotations into the sentences

- ❑ use literary present tense

Writing Workshop: Revising and Proofreading

DIRECTIONS The following literary analysis was written in response
to this prompt:

> **Write a literary analysis of a drama. Focus on either character,
> setting, imagery, theme, or symbolism.**

The literary analysis contains problems in style, content, and usage.

- Use the space between the lines to revise the essay and correct the
  errors.
- If you cannot fit some of your revisions between the lines, rewrite
  the revised sections on a separate piece of paper.

False Identity in *The Importance of Being Earnest*

Comedy frequently hinges on mistaken identity. In this play,

Oscar Wilde uses comedic characters to point out the theme that

society often requires people to be untruthful about their identities.

a. Problems with introduction

The two main male characters, Jack and Algernon, seek to protect

their reputations. To do so, they each assume the same false identity.

b. Problem with integration of quotation

Jack poses as Ernest when he is in London, in order to keep his

London life separate from his country life, where he is the guardian

of Cecily. Jack's words follow: "[I]n order to get up to town I have

always pretended to have a younger brother of the name of Ernest,

who . . . gets into the most dreadful scrapes" (Wilde 9–10). Under

this false identity, Jack courts Gwendolen when he is in London.

In order to meet Jack's ward, Cecily, Algernon also practices

deception. The troublemaking Algernon knows that Jack will pre-

vent him from meeting Cecily through normal social channels, so

Algernon secretly heads to the country, also pretending to be Ernest.

This false identity allows Algernon to establish a relationship with Cecily.

These gentlemen are not the only ones who create false identities. Their future wives, Gwendolen and Cecily, are not the docile creatures they appear to be. While pretending to be a dutiful daughter, Gwendolen actually does just as she pleases. Gwendolen has determined that she will marry whom she likes, whether or not he is acceptable to society or her mother. When her mother was out of the room, Gwendolen accepted Jack's proposal and then proceeded to blow kisses to him behind her mother's back (20).

c. Problem with use of literary present

Cecily is not what she seems, either. She may appear to be an innocent young girl, but she is actually quite passionate and romantic and given to interests other than her studies. She studies German grammar with a tutor, Mrs. Prism. Cecily is quite different from the prim schoolgirl that she pretends to be (34).

d. Problem with supporting detail

The characters in *The Importance of Being Earnest* use false identities to maneuver through society.

e. Problem with conclusion

Work Cited

Wilde, Oscar. *The Importance of Being Earnest*. Austin: Holt, Rinehart and Winston.

ELEMENTS OF LANGUAGE | Sixth Course

Reading Workshop: Literary Research Article

DIRECTIONS   Read the following passage, and answer the questions in the right-hand column.

Nigerian History as Background in *Things Fall Apart*

Published in 1958, two years before Nigeria's independence from British rule, Chinua Achebe's novel *Things Fall Apart* reflects political and social events of the Ibo people in what was to become Nigeria (Muoneke 40, 44). Set in the late 1800s when colonialists began imposing foreign cultures in West Africa, *Things Fall Apart* captures the complexities of colonization and tribal culture. Achebe highlights this period of history through a close-up look at one man.

Achebe begins the novel by illustrating the precolonial characteristics of the Ibo people: They are progressive, expansive, aggressive, adventurous, flexible, and tolerant. However, their flexibility and tolerance make their society vulnerable to outsiders (Njoku 29). Okonkwo, the novel's main character, represents an Ibo man's fame and power (Achebe 1). His experiences and the circumstances in which he finds himself provide a cultural and historical context for Nigeria before the arrival of the British colonials.

The second part of the novel reflects the period of colonial establishment when many Europeans arrived in West Africa to set up churches, a trading system, and a government (Killam 13, 15). Through the story of Okonkwo, Achebe illustrates the abuses some Nigerians faced as a result of colonization. During this period, the British began introducing imported goods, the English language, and the Anglican religion. When the Ibo began to resist these changes, the new government passed the Collective Punishment Ordinance of 1912. It enforced punishment for an entire village "if a crime were committed against a colonial officer, or if there were resistance to colonial rule, [with] no effort to identify the

1. What is the main idea of this paragraph?

____

____

____

____

2. In the second paragraph, what kinds of sources does the writer use?

____

____

____

____

3. What comparison is the writer making between events in the novel and the history of Nigeria?

____

____

____

____

individuals responsible" (Muoneke 41). This historical fact is represented in the novel when Okonkwo learns that the entire village of Abame has been massacred by British troops in retaliation for the murder of a missionary.

In the last section of *Things Fall Apart*, Okonkwo returns to his village, where events are escalating between the tribe and the colonial government. In retaliation for the mistreatment of Ibo elders, Okonkwo kills a chief messenger from the British court. When he learns his fellow villagers do not support his action, Okonkwo chooses to hang himself. His death represents the end of the old tribal society (Killam 15). According to Benedict Njoku:

> The tragedy of Okonkwo emanates from his resistance to change, from his imperviousness to the allurements of modernism born of European cultural traits. The disruption of Ibo traditional life is the last straw for him, hence his tragedy. (Njoku 17)

The three sections of *Things Fall Apart* represent the historical periods of precolonial, colonial, and post-colonial Nigeria. According to one reviewer, Achebe's account may even be considered historically accurate. Thus, Achebe traces the plight of an entire culture through the tragedy of Okonkwo.

Works Cited

Achebe, Chinua. *Things Fall Apart*. Austin: Holt, Rinehart and Winston.

Killam, G. D. *The Writings of Chinua Achebe*. London: Heinemann, 1977.

Muoneke, Romanus Okey. *Art, Rebellion and Redemption*. New York: Lang, 1994.

Njoku, Benedict Chiaka. *The Four Novels of Chinua Achebe*. New York: Lang, 1984.

4. What descriptions or minor details might be excluded from a summary of the fourth paragraph?

____

____

____

____

____

5. Why do you think the writer includes the quotation from Njoku in the fourth paragraph?

____

____

____

____

____

for **CHAPTER 26** `page 806` *continued*   **TEST**

DIRECTIONS Use the ideas and information in the third paragraph of the passage you have just read to complete the graphic organizer.

Summarizing

> **MAIN IDEA**

> **MAJOR SUPPORTING DETAILS**
>
> *In the novel, Okonkwo learns that the village of Abame was destroyed by the British because a missionary had been murdered.*

> **SUMMARY**

Writing Workshop: Literary Research Paper

DIRECTIONS Use the following revision guidelines to help you revise and correct the essay on the next page.

THE INTRODUCTION SHOULD

- hook the reader's attention

- give necessary background information

- state the thesis clearly

THE BODY SHOULD

- contain key ideas and specific details that relate directly to and support the thesis

- state facts and ideas mainly in the writer's own words

- use a variety of primary and secondary sources

- credit sources when necessary

THE CONCLUSION SHOULD

- restate the thesis

- end with some final insights

- include a *Works Cited* list

REMEMBER TO

- ❑ introduce quotations so that they fit smoothly into the paper

- ❑ punctuate quotations correctly

Writing Workshop: Revising and Proofreading

DIRECTIONS The following literary research paper was written in response to this prompt:

> **Write a formal research paper on a literary topic.**

This paper contains problems in style, content, and punctuation.

- Use the space between the lines to revise the paper and correct the errors.
- If you cannot fit your revisions between the lines, rewrite the revised sections on a separate piece of paper.

Evil Without Redemption in *Brighton Rock*

At 17, Pinkie, the main character in Graham Greene's 1938 novel *Brighton Rock,* is a traitor, a coward, and a murderer. However, he has grown up without material comfort or emotional support and the first murder he commits is an act of "justice" to avenge the death of his mentor. Unfortunately, Pinkie never recovers from the blows of injustice; the crimes he commits—and plans—overcome him.

Initially, Pinkie is clearly deprived of human sensibilities. The narrator often refers to Pinkie as the Boy. The narrator describes qualities that seem unnatural, like Pinkie's hatred of harmony and music, his "hideous and unnatural pride," and his "slatey eyes" that are "touched with the annihilating eternity from which he had come and to which he went" (Greene 4, 23). Even Pinkie proudly describes himself as an evil person: It's in the blood. Perhaps when they christened me, the holy water didn't take (Greene 169).

As the novel progresses, salvation is offered to Pinkie through Rose, a young woman who knows about his crime. Their proposed

<table>
<tr><td>a. Problem with relevancy of details</td></tr>
</table>

<table>
<tr><td>b. Problem with quotation punctuation</td></tr>
</table>

marriage—a convenient solution to covering a crime—is Pinkie's

chance to reject evil. Rose loves him unconditionally. Instead of

using his marriage to Rose as an opportunity for redemption, how-

ever, he turns it into his final crime—a complete betrayal of her love.

He attempts to induce Rose to kill herself.

In a reversal of his plans, he is trapped at the scene of the

attempted crime, faced with the people who have tracked him

down. "[H]ave I got to have a massacre?" (Greene 326) When he

finds that Rose has thrown away his gun, his face is transformed

into "a child's, badgered, confused, betrayed" (Greene 326). He

raises the bottle of acid he carries; a policeman smashes it and the

acid burns Pinkie's face. In pain, he runs off a cliff and drowns.

> **c.** Problem with quotation introduction

According to Greene,

The outlaw of justice always keeps in his heart the sense of

justice outraged. *His* crimes have an excuse and yet he is

pursued . . . Whatever crimes he may be driven to commit, the

child who doesn't grow up remains the great champion of jus-

tice (qtd. in Erdinast-Vulcan 18).

In the end, Pinkie is far from a hero.

> **d.** Problem with conclusion

Works Cited

Erdinast-Vulcan, Daphna. *Graham Greene's Childless Fathers.*

New York: St. Martin's, 1988.

Greene, Graham. *Brighton Rock.* London: Heinemann, 1938.

Reading Workshop: Persuasive Essay

DIRECTIONS Read the following passage, and answer the questions in the right-hand column.

Getting What You Pay For at National Parks

The United States' system of national parks is one of our country's most valuable jewels; from the coastline of Acadia in Maine to the tundra of the Gates of the Arctic in Alaska, our system of national parks preserves stunning scenery and important artifacts of our nation's history. However, maintenance has been deferred at many of the parks, and numerous park facilities need to be replaced or repaired. To care properly for our natural treasures, and to ensure that future generations can enjoy our national parks, the National Park Service should be allowed greater freedom in setting admission fees and in distributing the revenues generated from such fees.

A major source of funding for parks is admission fees, but until recently, a visit to a national park was an embarrassing bargain. At Yellowstone, Grand Teton, and Grand Canyon parks, fees were limited to $10 per vehicle or $5 per person, whichever was greater; and two-thirds of the National Park Service facilities charged no admission at all. A recreation-fee demonstration program that went into effect in 1997 allowed one hundred National Park Service sites to increase their fees. Yet, even with these increases, a family of four still pays more to see a first-run movie than they do for a week's entrance fees at Yellowstone National Park. How can an opportunity to see our precious national land be less valuable than a trip to the movies?

Although the federal government has been reluctant to charge for them, the government produces some goods and services for which consumers could and should pay. In fact, several government agencies, such as the Food and Drug Administration, the Patent and

1. What is the writer's opinion of the system of national parks?

____

____

____

____

2. Why do you think the writer includes the facts in the second paragraph?

____

____

____

____

3. How does the emotional appeal in the second paragraph support the writer's point of view?

____

____

____

____

Trademark Office, and the Securities and Exchange Commission already charge fees. Some of these fees cover the agencies' full cost of operations. Why shouldn't the National Park Service be allowed to raise fees to cover a larger part of its costs? The fear that national parks would become federal profit centers by charging exorbitant prices is unwarranted. National parks are in competition with one another and with privately owned amusement parks and recreation centers, and they can charge only what the market will bear.

The National Park Service should also be allowed to distribute its revenues among its parks according to the greatest need. Under the terms of the fee-demonstration program, 80 percent of admission fees stay in the park where they are collected. As a result, some of the most desperately needed repairs at smaller parks are neglected. A report from the U.S. General Accounting Office observes that sites not reaping the new revenue windfall may continue to see a multi-million-dollar maintenance backlog. The smaller parks, such as the George Washington Birthplace National Historic Site in Virginia or the Fort Davis National Historic Site in Texas, may not attract huge crowds, but they contain irreplaceable elements of our nation's culture and history, and they must be properly preserved.

Tying the hands of Park Service managers has allowed our national park system to languish in a state of disrepair and neglect. The National Park Service can take better care of our national treasures by reallocating funds and by raising admission fees at all parks. As an avid hiker and regular visitor to our nation's national parks, I believe that if we allow the parks to manage their own funds, we can enjoy these national treasures for generations to come.

4. What ethical appeal does the writer use in the fourth paragraph?

____

____

____

____

5. What does the writer seem to want readers to believe?

____

____

____

____

DIRECTIONS Use the ideas and information from the passage you have just read to complete the graphic organizer.

Identifying Point of View and Bias

1. What is the writer's background and experience?

The writer is a hiker who regularly visits national parks.

2. What connotative or loaded language does the essay contain?

3. Does the writer acknowledge opposing viewpoints? Explain.

4. What is the writer's point of view, and what biases might the writer have?

Writing Workshop: Persuasive Essay

DIRECTIONS Use the following guidelines to help you revise and correct the essay on the next page.

THE INTRODUCTION SHOULD

- capture the reader's attention

- provide necessary background information

- state the writer's position clearly and assertively

THE BODY SHOULD

- give at least three reasons to support the writer's position

- give at least two pieces of evidence for each reason

- contain appropriate logical, emotional, and ethical appeals

- concede or refute opposing positions

- be organized clearly and logically

THE CONCLUSION SHOULD

- restate the writer's position

- call readers to take action, if appropriate

REMEMBER TO

- ❏ repeat words and phrases to emphasize important points

- ❏ correct dangling modifiers

 TEST

Writing Workshop: Revising and Proofreading

DIRECTIONS The following persuasive essay was written in response to this prompt:

> **Write a persuasive essay defending a position that concerns the geographical area in which you live.**

The following essay contains problems in content, style, organization, and grammar.

- Use the space between the lines to revise the essay and correct the errors.
- If you cannot fit your revisions between the lines, rewrite the revised sections on a separate piece of paper.

Making the Range More Mellow

The traditional image of cattle herding involves some of the elements of a rodeo: dust flying, cowhands whooping, and nimble horses gathering up scattered cattle. That traditional method, however, is perhaps the least effective method of managing cattle in the open plains.

a. Problem with position statement

Consider the situation from the cows' point of view. Fleeing in terror from hollering cowhands is stressful. Acting less like cows' predators and more like their friends, "holistic herding" reduces stress on cattle. "Holistic herding" means that cowhands approach cattle, calmly and quietly, diagonally from the rear—never from cattle's blind spot, which is directly behind them. Cattle are guided when riders move into their space; riders then back off when cows take the hint. This calmer method of herding can even allow cattle to gain an extra pound a day.

b. Problem with dangling modifier

Cowhands have no need to carry prods or heavy leather whips. In addition, they do not have to exert as much physical and emotional energy to do their jobs. Although the instinct to want to shove cattle is hard to overcome, young cowhands are quickly learning that they do not have to spend their days punching cattle and getting just as mad as the cows they are poking and prodding.

c. Problem with lack of reason

"Holistic herding" is also less stressful on the environment. Vegetation around streambeds can recover far more quickly when it is walked on by a herd of cattle than when it is churned by racing hooves.

d. Problem with organization in paragraphs

"Holistic herding" is not a new, untried technique. The idea of cooperating with animals instead of frightening them is fairly simple, and it was practiced until the advent of the great cattle drives of the Old West. Pastures benefit when cattle are moved more easily because overgrazing is reduced. It has been revived by some wise modern ranchers, who are reaping the benefits of this low-tech idea.

More ranchers should consider adopting "holistic herding," which requires no expensive equipment or training. The technique can reduce overgrazing, streambed erosion, and stress levels.

e. Problem with lack of repetition for emphasis

Reading Workshop: Review of a Documentary

DIRECTIONS Read the following passage, and answer the questions in the right-hand column.

Team Effort

"Who cares about ballroom dance?" I groaned, getting my last choice of documentaries for this assignment. I had hoped for one of the movies about basketball, such as *Hoop Dreams*, but they were all already taken. I ended up with *Mad Hot Ballroom*, which is about fifth graders in a ballroom dance competition. Who cares about a bunch of little kids dancing around? It turns out I do, because the kids in *Mad Hot Ballroom* discover something crucial for basketball or any other group project: how to give it your all for the team.

In this absorbing film by Marilyn Agrelo and Amy Sewell, we follow three groups of fifth graders in New York City who take a mandatory class in ballroom dancing, leading up to a competition among schools from all over the city. In competition, teams of several pairs of dancers earn points for style, getting the steps right, and partnering well. The dancers are ten or eleven years old—not "little kids" anymore (though still embarrassed by holding hands in public) but not yet too guarded to let us see what they think. Part of the charm of this movie is being included in their frank discussions about what they like, what they hate, what they worry about, and what they want to do when they grow up.

Agrelo and Sewell reveal the young students to us in two ways: by interviewing the kids on camera, and by filming them as they practice, walk to school, and talk to friends. At first, they seem skeptical about learning dance, but they get more and more enthusiastic as they find out how much fun they have when they've mastered it. By having them both "show" us and "tell" us in their own words, the filmmakers let viewers experience the kids' realization that to

1. Why does this writer initially think she would not be interested in this documentary?

____

____

____

____

2. What descriptive words in the second paragraph signal the author's opinion?

____

____

____

____

____

3. What two documentary filming techniques does the writer discuss? Explain.

____

____

____

____

____

win the competition, they have to get over their embarrassment, work together, and practice harder than they have ever practiced anything before. My basketball coach calls this "giving a hundred and ten percent for the team," and though that's an old cliché, it evokes working a little harder than you thought you could—not to make yourself look good, but for the team. *Mad Hot Ballroom* lets us relive the first time we figured this out for ourselves.

One boy in the film, Cyrus, describes team effort vividly. After his team loses the semifinals, a judge tells the devastated kids that another school won by only three points. At first, Cyrus doesn't understand why his team didn't win when they wanted it so much, as if wanting should be enough. Later, though, he tells his class-mates he's realized that if every dancer had done just one thing a lit-tle better, the team would have won—and that he knows he could have done at least one thing better himself.

In contrast to Cyrus, another student resists teamwork. Tall for his age and handsome, Jonathan is a natural dancer but won't let anyone, including the dance teacher, tell him what to do. He goofs around during practice. He's rude to a teammate, a shy kid who might be the only boy on the team more talented than he is, and has to be forced to apologize. Just days before the competition, the teacher orders him to shape up or be kicked off the team. He quits. In an interview, Jonathan explains that he "only really cares about basketball," as though that excuses letting his teammates down. We see him on the basketball court with friends, hogging the ball for lay-ups, not passing. His story provides a vivid contrast to the engaging insights many of the other young dancers develop.

Whatever the sport, good players on any team know they have to "give a hundred and ten percent for the team" to win. Anyone who understands this will find it fascinating to watch the subjects of this film learn it for the first time.

4. What does Jonathan con-tribute to the documen-tary?

____

____

____

____

5. What does the writer think of Agrelo and Sewell's doc-umentary?

____

____

____

____

ELEMENTS OF LANGUAGE | Sixth Course

DIRECTIONS Use the ideas and information in the passage you have just read to complete the graphic organizer.

Identifying Criteria for Evaluation

▶ CRITERIA	▶ EVALUATION	▶ EVIDENCE
The information is presented in a way that is accessible and engaging.	*Yes, the reviewer finds the subjects of the film appealing. The reviewer thinks the documentary gives viewers a look at an interesting part of their development, when they discover the value (and difficulty) of teamwork. She suggests that viewers will identify with them.*	
The documentary provides accurate and comprehensive information from authoritative sources.		
The audio and visual components work in concert to create a certain effect, whether dramatic, provocative, or comedic.		*"Agrelo and Sewell reveal them to us in two ways: by interviewing the kids on camera, and by filming them as they practice, walk to school, and talk to friends. . . . By having them both "show" us and "tell" us in their own words, the filmmakers let viewers experience the kids' realization . . ."*

Writing Workshop: Review of a Documentary

DIRECTIONS Use the following guidelines to help you revise and correct the essay on the next page.

THE INTRODUCTION SHOULD

- hook the reader
- persuasively state the reviewer's overall opinion of the documentary
- provide background information

THE BODY SHOULD

- give criteria-based reasons to support the opinion
- support each reason with evidence
- effectively organize the review

THE CONCLUSION SHOULD

- restate the opinion
- urge readers either to see or to avoid the documentary
- offer a concluding thought that goes beyond the thesis

REMEMBER TO

- ❑ avoid unnecessary words and phrases
- ❑ avoid sentence fragments

Writing Workshop: Revising and Proofreading

DIRECTIONS The documentary review was written in response to the following prompt:

Review a documentary film you have seen.

The review contains problems in content, style, and grammar.

- Use the space between the lines to revise the errors and improve the style.
- If you cannot fit some of your revisions between the lines, rewrite the revised sections on a separate piece of paper.

Maya Lin: A Strong Clear Vision

Since its construction, the stark beauty of the Vietnam Veterans

Memorial in Washington D.C., has proved to be unforgettable. Its

long, dark walls have helped visitors come to terms with their per-

sonal grief and loss. The documentary *Maya Lin: A Strong Clear*

Vision, by Freida Lee Mock, tells the story of the controversy sur-

rounding artist Maya Lin and her design for the Memorial.

a. Problem with opinion statement

By poignantly highlighting the passionate feelings of veterans

and politicians who opposed the design. Mock's documentary edu-

cates Americans about an important part of their history. Mock

b. Problem with sentence fragments

weaves together news footage with in-depth interviews to trace the

arguments raised against Lin and her unorthodox design. When Lin

entered the national competition that chose the Memorial's design.

She submitted a plan that was nothing like a traditional statue: She

proposed to cut a wedge in the ground and bury in it two horizon-

tal granite walls. On the walls' polished black surfaces would be

inscribed the names of the nearly 60,000 men and women who were killed during, or are still missing from, the Vietnam War. In grainy

news footage, the courageous young designer staunchly defends the

integrity of her design, which opponents dismissed as "insulting

and depressing."

Although the focus of the documentary is the "strong clear

vision," Mock allows viewers a revealing, though incomplete,

glimpse into the strength and sincerity of the artist's character. Mock

shows how Lin herself came under attack after her design was cho-

sen from the 1,441 entries in the competition. When she won over

some of the most respected architecture firms in the country, she

was a student at Yale—a young Asian woman whose design was

part of a class project. In defense of her unique and original design,

Lin explains to Americans that the Memorial asks them to examine

the war, honestly and painfully, without looking away: "So what the

Memorial's about is honesty. . . . You have to accept, and admit that

this pain has occurred, in order for it to be healed." I think that

noticeably absent from the documentary is a close-up look at Lin's

personality or the events that helped shape her ideas. To understand

the artist, Mock seems to say, examine her work.

Although the documentary leaves viewers wanting to know

more about Lin, it brings to light an important national discussion

that becomes part of the healing process the Memorial was designed

to aid.

> **c.** Problems with unneces-
> sary words

> **d.** Problem with
> recommendation

Reading Workshop: Proposal

DIRECTIONS Read the following article, and answer the questions in the right-hand column.

Putting a Driver in the Driver's Seat

School bus drivers are becoming harder and harder to find for most districts. Nationwide, the number of available drivers is at a 20 percent shortfall. Officials in forty-four states cite a shortage of drivers; seventeen states declare the problem to be severe. The situation is causing canceled field trips and athletic events as well as long waits for rides to school.

The main reason for the shortage is the country's robust economy. With low pay for heavy responsibilities, the job holds little attraction for workers. Many former drivers have found more lucrative jobs elsewhere. Few new workers are drawn to a job that has traditionally offered no benefits packages and at the same time carries such high risks. Controlling a bus full of children while safely operating a vehicle is a challenge not many are willing to face for so few benefits.

While the causes of the problem are easy to understand, solutions are hard to find. School districts have attempted to ease the driver shortage in several ways. Some districts have offered signing bonuses and higher wages, increased the number of hours available to drivers, and offered benefits like child care. When districts offer training for drivers to receive commercial licenses, they can only watch as the recruits leave for higher-paying work in trucking. Districts seek recruits at job fairs and through television and radio ads, but all their efforts are proving to be ineffective.

To solve this busing problem, school districts should borrow a more creative solution from transportation experts. For example, many communities encourage car pooling by providing vans for large groups of commuters. Schools could provide a few vans to

1. What are some of the effects of the bus driver shortage?

____

____

____

____

2. Based on this article and your own knowledge, what is another generalization you can make about the problems caused by a driver shortage?

____

____

____

____

3. Which paragraph discusses the background of the problem? What does it explain?

____

____

____

____

parents to supplement their busing programs. The vans might even prove to be cost-effective since parents would drive them, saving schools the drivers' salaries.

Parents could rotate driving responsibilities with other parents on a volunteer basis. No special license or training would be required; only a safe driving record and an insurance waiver would be necessary. Of course, some parents would be unable or unwilling to drive a van. However, because most parents are inconvenienced when their children don't have rides to school and school events, cooperation is very likely. Some sacrifice would be required of all participating parents, but careful planning would minimize the sacrifice of time and maximize the benefits of reliable transportation.

Ideally, attracting more qualified drivers could solve the bus driver shortage; however, that solution has not yet been effective. The best means of dealing with this problem is to get assistance from people who are affected by it and willing to help. Provide parents with the appropriate vehicles, and they will make sure that their children arrive safely and on time to school and extracurricular functions.

4. What is one advantage to the solution offered in this proposal?

____

____

____

____

5. What is a possible drawback to the solution?

____

____

____

____

DIRECTIONS Complete the graphic organizer below. Identify the paragraphs in which each part of the problem-solution structure is located, and write the numbers of the paragraphs in the spaces provided. Write brief summaries of each part of the essay.

Analyzing Problem-Solution Structure

PROBLEM (PARAGRAPH (S) 1)

In many school districts in the country, there is a shortage of bus drivers to provide transportation to students.

BACKGROUND INFORMATION (PARAGRAPH(S) _______)

POSSIBLE SOLUTIONS: ADVANTAGES/DISADVANTAGES (PARAGRAPH(S)_______)

PROPOSAL OF BEST SOLUTION (PARAGRAPH(S)_______)

Writing Workshop: Proposal

DIRECTIONS Use the following guidelines to help you revise and correct the essay on the next page.

THE INTRODUCTION SHOULD

- immediately get readers interested in the problem

- clearly state the problem

- give background information

- include a clear thesis statement with a proposed solution to the problem

THE BODY SHOULD

- include a brief discussion of other possible solutions

- clearly discuss the recommended solution and the process for implementing it

- discuss possible objections to the proposed solution

- persuade readers by refuting possible objections to the proposed solution

THE CONCLUSION SHOULD

- restate the thesis

- end with a call to action, if appropriate

REMEMBER TO

- ❑ avoid overusing passive voice

- ❑ utilize commas properly with subordinate adverb clauses

Writing Workshop: Revising and Proofreading

DIRECTIONS The following proposal was written in response to this prompt:

What can be done to prevent summer power shortages?

The essay contains problems in content, style, and punctuation.

- Use the space between the lines to revise the proposal and correct the errors.
- If you cannot fit some of your revisions between the lines, rewrite the revised sections on a separate piece of paper.

"Unplugging" Prevents Summer Power Shortages

As summer temperatures climb, we try to avoid the heat by staying in climate-controlled spaces. Consequently, energy usage soars when everyone turns on fans and air conditioners. Increasingly, utility companies can't keep up when entire cities try to escape from a heat wave. As a result, power can shut down completely.

a. Problem with thesis

A heat wave in 1999 left 68,000 people in New York City without electric power for days. As the temperature reached 101 degrees, subway service temporarily shut down, food spoiled in refrigerators, and people slept on the streets, seeking cooler air. When temperatures and power usage climb, cities have a limited number of ways to avert power shortages. Although cities can find ways to generate more electricity they are expensive; constructing dams, generators, or coal-burning plants can cost millions of dollars. In addition, power plants take years to construct.

b. Problem with punctuation

Instead, cities and their citizens should find ways to *reduce* usage of the already-available energy. There are dozens of effective conservation ideas, from planting trees to installing energy-saving light bulbs. However, these ideas can take years to be effective, and they do not offer enough help during peak periods.

A program that automatically "unplugs" appliances may be a simple answer to power shortages. This program, which would attach timers to hot-water heaters and radio receivers to air-conditioning compressors, was developed by electric utility companies. The appliances would be briefly turned off by the timers during peak demand time, between 5 P.M. and 6 P.M. The timers, either mechanically set or activated by a radio signal, would be attached by the utility company. Service would be interrupted by the timers for up to fifteen minutes during peak periods, but the interruption would be virtually unnoticeable to customers.

c. Problems with passive voice

Some critics may argue that such a program is unnecessary because people can turn off their appliances whenever they want.

d. Problem with objection

The "unplugged utilities" program benefits everyone involved. The residents who participate in the program will see their utility bills decrease from reduced consumption. Their bills can be lowered even more, because utility companies generally offer a monthly credit to users who participate. If consumption is reduced, utility companies can avoid adding expensive power plants to their systems. Most importantly, reduced consumption ensures that expensive, uncomfortable summer blackouts can become a thing of the past.